BEYOND BASEBALL

Daniel Venn

Rounding First

Foreword by Marvin Benard

Cover Art by: DnJCards
Artist Contact: DnJCards@Outlook.com

ISBN: 0692692398
ISBN-13: 978-0692692394

World Beyond Publishing

Acknowledgments

In memory of Lee Bjorkman

Craig—Thank you for the opportunity, the adventure, and for being so good-natured in response to me writing down our stories. In our broken Spanish, "usted es hombre".

Jay and Scott—I couldn't have asked for better men to travel with. The work you choose to do for Nicaragua is incredible and inspiring.

Sergio, Luis, Orvin, Jonathan—Thank you for making everything possible and getting us back home in (mostly) one piece.

A special thanks to the following individuals for sharing their stories, experiences, and insights: Marvin Benard, Ruby Rojas, Roniel Raudes, Marlon Avea, Kevin Gadea, Bob Oettinger, Nick Holmes II, Johnny Alvarez.

Beyond Baseball

Foreword

I dug in against Mike Fetters in the bottom of the ninth. Even though there were forty thousand in the stands, the place had gone nearly silent when the Dodgers came back from a four-run deficit to tie the game. The Giants hate the Dodgers, and the Dodgers hate the Giants, and it's been that way for a long time. I grew up a Dodgers fan, so playing against them on Sunday Night Baseball was special to me for more than the rivalry. Fetters had been great that year, especially against lefties, so I was just trying to do my job as our leadoff hitter and get on base. With two strikes, he tried to come inside with a fastball but missed out over the plate. I put a good swing on it and watched as the ball cleared the fence in right center. Game over.

I grew up in Nicaragua and had a great childhood there. Everyone knew everyone in my town, and there were many other kids my age to play with. However, my family didn't have much, and I couldn't have dreamed that someday I'd be jumping into a mob of my teammates at home plate after hitting a walk off against my favorite team on national TV. Growing up, I didn't have many opportunities in baseball, definitely not enough to think I would ever be able to play the game professionally. As a kid, I was only able to play one year of little league in Nicaragua, and even then, we rarely played more than once a week. Finding equipment was always difficult. I cannot remember a time when we didn't have to share equipment, which was particularly difficult for me being left-handed.

Many challenges face baseball players in Nicaragua. Much like my family growing up, many families lack the resources and money for their children to play baseball. Teams of all levels struggle to afford basic equipment, let alone good equipment. Because the pay is so little, it is hard to find good coaches, leaving players with a limited understanding of the game. Many young players don't know how to hit cutoff men, keep the double play in order, or move runners over offensively. All of these problems perpetuate each other, making it very difficult for Nicaraguan players to find success in baseball.

There is a great need for donated baseball equipment at all levels in Nicaragua, but especially for kids. Baseball equipment can be life-changing for young players. For a child who has never owned a decent glove, bat, or even a ball, getting these items can provide them opportunities in the game they never dreamed possible. As important as equipment donations are, helping to provide proper nutrition for kids is also vital in Nicaragua. While helping at clinics, I've noticed that many kids arrive hungry, not having eaten breakfast or lunch. Bringing both baseball equipment and food to Nicaragua has the potential to do so much good.

I decided to return to Nicaragua to coach the national team in the World Baseball Classic because I want to give back to the game that has done so much for me. I love baseball, and I love Nicaragua, and I want to see players from my country have the chance to succeed on the biggest stages. Baseball gives children hope in Nicaragua, and hope is motivating. Baseball has the potential to change the lives of young players here, and equipment donations from charities like Helping Kids Round First helps make that possible.

-Marvin Benard

Prologue

Of all the airports in all the cities in the world. Of all the days in all the months on the calendar. Here I am, desperately trying to run as far from my problems as I can, and fate is just sitting here laughing at me.

I tried to find out what there was beyond baseball. I really gave it a go. Ecuador, the Galapagos, Peru. Heck, even the remote Samoan Islands. I went to the kinds of places where I would pull out my glove and the ball I always found room for in my suitcase and toss it to one of the kids I taught and they'd just drop it on the ground and kick it back and forth with their friends.

I even took my host father in Ecuador out in the front yard and handed him a glove, trying to bond with him in the most American father-son way possible: having a catch. He put the glove on his right hand, put the ball in the glove, and tried to use the glove to hurl it at me. He thought baseball was lacrosse.

I came home and got a stable job teaching kids a bunch of meaningless history trivia they'll never need to know. A real big boy job. I even bought myself a suit and some ties.

I got myself a bank account to put my paychecks in. I found a nice girl to spend them on. I stopped drinking like a college student, and when I did drink, I used a bottle opener and poured into a glass. I started watching the news instead of Baseball Tonight. I made CNN my computer homepage, ESPN finally being displaced.

I started tucking in my shirt. Not just when I went to work, but when I went places like the grocery store. Heck, I went places like the grocery store!

And here I am. Broke, unemployed, luckless, loveless, sitting in an airport lobby at one in the morning, a couple t-shirts and my baseball glove stuffed into a backpack on the bench next to me. It took me fifteen hours to get from Denver to Minneapolis yesterday, going from my sister's basement where I had been staying to my parents' where all my stuff is, to hastily pack my bag. Five more hours and I was in Sioux Falls, rubbing sleep out of my eyes, way too early at the airport. Six more hours and my flight will leave.

I have no plan. I have no money. There is nothing rational about what I'm doing. This is not how a college-educated professional acts in the real world. But there's baseball on the other end and no place I'd rather be.

I had half a mind, maybe more, to just delete the email a few words in. Those Nigerian princes that always want to deposit a few millions dollars in my bank account write in better English.

"We've grown. Many projects. 1st ocean container at Managua. Baseball gear. Waiting for government. Will distribute around country. Not looking as many

people involved, but you seem to have passion for this.
We farm now, ship hospitals, etc. Baseball opened
doors. Interested?"

Don't do this, my head pleaded. You've got a job.
We could even call it a career. You read the newspaper.
You cook for yourself. You do your own laundry. Don't
give all that up.

My hands reached for my phone anyways despite
the compelling, boring argument my head was making.
I stared at the last line while I waited for someone to
pick up. *Baseball opened doors.* It had spent the last
decade holding doors open for me, shoving me through
them when I'd protest, then rushing to beat me to the
next door in time to get it opened up in front of me.

I simply said yes to every question the man on the
other side of the phone asked. Yes, I was interested in
their projects. Yes, I was willing to travel. Yes, I could
open up my schedule if necessary. Yes, I was up to date
with all my vaccines and immunizations.

Sure, you've opened up enough doors for me,
baseball, I thought when I hung up the phone. Now let's
see if you can save my life.

I was feeling pretty confident about it until last
night when she messaged me. Two months of free fall
rushed through my mind as soon as I saw her name on
the screen. Then the last year and a half followed.
"Hey! I'll be home tomorrow. Want to get coffee? I've
got a long layover in Atlanta, so I'll get in touch then to
set something up. I want to see you when I get back."
I checked my boarding passes. Sioux Falls to Atlanta.
Nine hour layover. Then Atlanta to Nicaragua.

Here I am, trying to run as far away from my
problems as possible, and they'll be waiting for me in

the airport.

How do you respond to that message? The girl I had settled down for. The girl I had left the Peace Corps for. The girl I had turned down the dream job writing baseball for because it would have moved me away from her. The girl who had our wedding planned, our house picked out, our kids named.

The girl who had disappeared. No explanation. Just silence. Two whole months of silence. Agonizing, oppressive silence. Silence that settles into your bones and drives you crazy, crazy probably being an understatement.

And now, the night before I leave on the trip to get away from her, to forget her, to move on from her, she comes walking out of the cornfield wanting to have a catch.

I still haven't responded. Her message is still open on my phone, taunting me, when I go to check the time. I've been checking the time a lot tonight. I hope it's not because I want to read her words again.

Let me say right now, I was going to keep this book clean and professional. Cut out all the cuss words, smut, and bathroom humor from the first one. To be Ricky Vaughn in Major League II, with his act cleaned up, respectable, and not Wild Thing. To handle it all with tact and eloquence.

But, I've got to say, fate, this is a real pisser.

Anyways. Eat your heart out, real world

Chapter 1

You get a different kind of sick when you're abroad. You haven't traveled until you've found yourself in the fetal position on a dirt bathroom floor spooning the toilet, unsure what end of you fluid is going to leak out of next. Until you've crapped yourself on the sidewalk in Costa Rica and then blamed it on the family dog, breakfast running down the inside of your leg and seeping into your tennis shoes.

We haven't even left the country and I'm already making mad dashes into airport bathrooms. Thankfully, I know I haven't caught some contagious, killer foreign disease yet. No, this morning I have a case of Busch Light. Well, last night I had a case of Busch Light. Regardless.

I knew it was irresponsible, but when your college roommate of three years, already letting you crash at his place and driving you to the airport in the middle of the night, tells you he's getting married and he'd like you to be a groomsman, you toss back cans of cheap beer like you're back in the freshmen dorms together.

I have no idea why he wants me to be in his wedding. Heck, I have no idea why he'd even risk having me attend. After three years of living with me, cleaning up after me, doing my dishes, carrying me up the stairs and tucking me in when I found myself unable, you'd think he'd be trying to keep me as far away from the most important day of his life as possible.

I was always *that* friend in college. The one whose stories you loved to hear the morning after, shaking your head. The one whose escapades you loved to watch from a safe distance and laugh at while also feeling thankful that you weren't involved. The one you were entertained by but also felt sorry for.

I've really done some growing up since. I more or less stopped drinking after graduation, at least at college levels. But an exception must be made for an engagement.

There aren't many things worse than a nine-hour layover. Being hungover for a nine-hour layover and knowing that the ex-girlfriend you're still insane about is somewhere in the same airport is one of those things.

I'm sure Craig and Jay, the two middle-aged gentlemen who run the non-profit sponsoring this trip, are regretting not putting me through a more comprehensive vetting process before agreeing to take me along. Here I am, red-eyed, mumbling, repeatedly running to the bathroom. Talk about first impressions.

Not to mention my constant glances over my shoulder, my eyes frantically darting from face-to-face, hoping one will be hers while also praying desperately that I don't find her.

If a TSA agent happens to see me, I fully expect to

be dragged into some back interrogation room. I'm unkempt and disheveled, suspiciously looking every which way, exactly the kind of person chosen for a not-so-random inspection.

I've only been in one of those back interrogation rooms one time. Leaving Samoa, minding my own business and moping about giving up and going home from the Peace Corps for a girl, two beefy Samoan police officers appeared at my sides, arms crossed. Beefy was probably redundant there, given Samoa's ascension as a recruiting hot spot for NFL lineman due to their propensity to grow 6'5, 300 lb men, women, and children. These two cops had clearly drank the water growing up.

"Are you Daniel Venn?" one asked through a thick Samoan accent. Wide-eyed, I confirmed that I was.

"Did you pack your own bag?" I had.

"Come with us." They escorted me through the airport lobby, curious heads of other travelers turning to watch me, one guard on each side of me, each holding on to one of my arms.

We arrived at a small room in the bowels of the airport. My suitcase sat on a small metal table surrounded by hulking Samoan police officers and airport guards. Two were in swat gear, automatic rifles held across their chests.

"Is this your bag?" one of my escorts demanded. I thought about lying, saying it wasn't. There wasn't anything in there worth staying in this situation for. Even without their rifles, the sheer size of the officers was enough to keep me honest. I nodded.

"Do you understand that it is illegal to transport dangerous weapons through our airport, punishable by imprisonment?"

I was stammering that there must have been a misunderstanding when he handed me an x-ray printout of my bag, his finger pointing to a long blade at the bottom of my bag.

My machete. My dad had presented it to me the night before I left. "You know, for coconuts!"

"Can you explain to us why you have an 18-inch steel blade in your suitcase?" the officer asked, his tone making me either want to break for the nearest exit or wet my pants.

"You know, for coconuts?"

The guards huddled, talking loudly in Samoan. I wished I had paid more attention in our language classes. I hadn't stayed long enough in the country to learn more than "Hello", "Goodbye", and "Help! I'm being attacked by dogs!", a pretty useful phrase in a country where the number one reason Peace Corp Volunteers end up in the hospital is dog bites.

"Can we see it?" one of the armed guards asked. It was a question, but I knew I didn't have a choice.

I'd much prefer if you would just kill me with your guns, I thought. *Much quicker and less painful for me. Less mess for you, too! Win-win!* Instead, I just nodded feebly.

He descended on my bag, tossing clothes and belongings aside, no attention paid to my meticulous pack job. He found the machete only after removing everything from my bag and tossing it asunder on the floor around him.

The guards began talking loudly and rapidly in Samoan again, snatching the machete out of each other's hands.

They're debating which one gets to kill me, I thought. I started surveying them, debating which looked the strongest and would be able to remove my head most efficiently and painlessly.

The machete ended up in the hands of the original monster officer who had confronted me in the lobby. He pulled the black protective sheath off the machete, exposing the long silver blade.

How does this work? Do I get on my knees? Do they put a bag over my head? I've never been executed before!

The officer ran his fingers the length of the blade.

"Very sharp!" he said, turning it over in his hands. He grasped it at both ends and tried to bend it. "Very strong!" He handed it to the guard next to him, who went through the same routine before passing it off. It made its way around the circle before returning to the hands of the first guard. He put the sheath back over the blade and held it out to me.

"Very nice *sapelu*! Thank you for letting us see it!" With that, the guards filed out of the room, leaving me to pick up my belongings, thank the good Lord for my safety, and find myself a new pair of pants.

Following my scare in Samoa and having watched enough Locked Up Abroad on TV to be terrified of walking out my own front door, I was skeptical when Craig pulled into the airport at four AM and handed me three suitcases.

"You'll check these," he said after we had introduced ourselves. He was in his early sixties, a mammoth of a man with a booming voice and exaggerated features.

Sure, I thought. *Give the new guy the luggage with*

*all the drugs in them. I'll be rotting away in some
Nicaraguan jail while you sip rum on the beach.*

When his back was turned, saying farewell to his
wife who had dropped him off at the airport, I unzipped
one of the suitcases. Brand new pearl white baseballs
sat tucked into a pile of baseball gloves, their original
tags still attached.

"We've got seven suitcases full," Craig said as the
gear spilled onto my lap. "Not to mention, over six
thousand balls, eight hundred gloves, fourteen hundred
bats, seven hundred helmets, and thousands of jerseys
sitting in a warehouse waiting for us in Managua."

Our first flight took us from Sioux Falls to Atlanta.
I was asleep before the plane left the ground and didn't
wake up until we touched down again. During our
layover in Atlanta that afternoon, Craig spread a large
map of Nicaragua across a table in front of us and
haphazardly traced the routes we could take across
Nicaragua with a finger. The more roads he traced, the
more cities we could reach, the more excited he got.
Our trip would take us from Managua, the capital city
of Nicaragua sitting on the southwest tip of Lake
Managua, to the southernmost cities in Nicaragua:
Rivas, San Juan del Sur, and the Island of Omotepe in
the middle of Lake Nicaragua. I had been to San Juan
del Sur, a beautiful city squeezed between the Pacific
Ocean and Lake Nicaragua, on my first trip to
Nicaragua years earlier. Our team of American
ballplayers had driven up from Costa Rica to play a
series of games at a baseball academy outside of Rivas,
staying at a hostel in San Juan del Sur each night.

I was excited to go back. Some of the best
ballplayers I had ever played against had been at that

academy near Rivas, teenage kids throwing mid-90s fastballs. The field sat on the shores of Lake Nicaragua, the twin volcanoes on the Island of Ometepe towering over the outfield, warm lake breezes sweeping over the field, a line of palm trees separating the field from one of the largest freshwater lakes in the world.

After our games at the academy, we'd retreated back to San Juan del Sur, a city stretched around a horseshoe bay on the ocean, beach reaching as far as the eye could see in both directions. The largest statue of Christ in Central America stood on a bluff overlooking the bay and the city, one arm outstretched in blessing. I had learned to surf there. Each night, we sat on the beach with bottles of Flor de Caña rum in one hand and fat hand-rolled cigars in the other, watching the sun set over the bay.

Beyond all the warm memories, I also had revenge on the mind in my return to San Juan del Sur. All the fun and games had been cut short for me on our first trip when I was attacked at our hostel the morning I was scheduled to pitch against the team at the academy. Up early trying to get my head right, my game face on, trying to forget the size, athleticism, and power the teenagers at the academy had displayed against us the previous day, minding my own business by the hostel's pool, the pet monkey that lived on the roof of the hostel had swooped down onto my lap and bit me on the hand. My hand had quickly swelled up to cartoonish proportions, making it impossible for me to pitch that afternoon. I still have the scar to this day, one I'm not above showing off to girls at parties.

I'm coming for you, Buzz the Monkey, I thought as Craig's finger circled San Juan del Sur on the map.

Following the southern portion of our trip, we would venture north with baseball gear. Craig pointed out the cities of León, Chinandega, Somotillo, Jinotega, and Somoto on his map, all places at which communities and teams were waiting to receive equipment. If there was enough time, we would also head east, winding around Lake Nicaragua and taking a spider web of roads, possibly making it as far as the Caribbean Sea. Our trip would span from the Costa Rican border in southern Nicaragua to the Honduran border in the north, from the Pacific Ocean across the country to the Atlantic, bringing children the opportunity to play baseball at every stop along the way.

Following our planning session, I wandered the airport aimlessly, looking up flights leaving to Minneapolis on the big board, letting myself walk until the gate she may be at came into sight, then panicking and turning around. What would I even say if I found her? I had only seen her one time in the past two months, at Christmas, trying to drop presents for her and her family off at her door. She had simply spit "What are you doing here?" at me when she saw me at the door, and I feared I couldn't expect any more kind of a reception here in the airport.

Eventually, we boarded our flight to Managua and were in the air. Craig and I talked for the entirety of the flight. I was fascinated.

Here he was, at sixty-three years old he'd recently quit a cushy, presidentially-appointed job to devote his time to hauling baseball equipment to kids in Nicaragua. When he was my age, he had already been around the world and back again, hopping buses and trains and ships across Europe, Central and South America, and Asia, doing business on the streets and in markets of the countries he traveled to, making just enough money to afford a place to sleep at night and then move on.

His stories took me along with him from Mexico to Australia to Israel to England while our plane took me from the United States to Nicaragua. Upon arrival, as we were grabbing our carry-on luggage from the overhead, he said, hushed, "At security, if I tell you to move, just leave the bags and go. Fast. We have thousands of dollars of brand new, in the package baseball gear with us and it's very likely they'll think we're here to make money. So if I say go, do it. Let's not end up in jail on our first night."

Gulp.

Of course, as we approached the security area, me trembling with fear already, our seven bags of possibly illicit baseball equipment being pushed in a cart in front of me, he told me that I'd have to handle the conversations with the security and border agents since I spoke the best Spanish.

"Sometimes you just have to work the system. If we have to meet a guard in the parking lot and give him a glove and a bat and a hundred dollar bill in exchange for letting us through, it's worth it to get all the rest of the gear into the hands of children." He made it sound like it had happened before.

We passed through the passport check quickly, guards simply glancing at our documents and waiving us through, and approached the baggage check. We were instructed to load our bags onto large X-ray scanners and crossed our fingers.

"That one," a border agent said pointing at our first bag. "And that one too. And that one. All of them. All of it needs to be searched." He waved to a nearby security guard. My heart nearly stopped.

"Remember, if I say go, just go," Craig whispered in my ear as we carted our bags over to the inspection table, the security guard now at our side.

"The books!" Jay whispered into my other ear. He hadn't been seated near Craig and me on either of our flights, and I hadn't gotten the chance to talk to him much yet. He was a diminutive man, quiet, a stark contrast to Craig's gigantic personality. He hadn't spoken up often during our planning session in the airport, but when he had, his ideas were always constructive and helpful. This was no exception. "Let them search the books first."

He had brought a suitcase full of picture books in English and Spanish to be donated to a daycare they had visited on a previous trip. When we reached the inspection table, a pair of border agents on the other side, we placed Jay's suitcase of books in front of one of the agents, Craig's personal bag of clothes in front of the other. They opened both and began rifling through.

"Books. Books. It's just books and candy," one guard said to the other in Spanish, holding up a copy of *The Hungry, Hungry Caterpillar*. The other was holding up a pair of Craig's underwear, a confused look on his face.

"It's all for children," I said, trying to remember Spanish I hadn't used in years. "Well, except those." I pointed to Craig's underwear, still in the hands of the bewildered guard. They didn't laugh. I grabbed Craig's passport from the table and showed the guards page after page of Nicaraguan border stamps. "We are a charity organization named Helping Kids Round First. We come here often. Everything is for the children of Nicaragua." My sentences were short and choppy, my Spanish rusty.

They pushed Craig's personal bag aside and motioned for us to put another bag on the table. Jay handed his personal suitcase to them. Only my bag stood between us and having our bags of baseball gear searched and probably seized. There were more than one hundred brand new Spalding gloves inside of them, as well as hundreds of brand new baseballs. The retail value of the cargo easily exceeded ten thousand dollars. Even if they allowed us to keep the gear, the taxes levied on them would be crippling to our trip.

Craig was nervously reading a picture book to the guard with the bag of books, showing that it was in Spanish and English and repeating "For the children!" between lines in broken Spanish. I continued pleading our case to the guard now looking through Jay's bag. When he began pulling out Jay's underwear, an exasperated *Oh, not again!* look came across his face. He put the underwear back.

"Go," he said in English, pointing to the exit of the airport. We didn't even take the time to zip the bags that had been on the table closed, tossing them back onto our cart as quickly as we could and heading for the exit before the guards could change their minds.

We didn't speak until we were outside in the warm Nicaraguan night air.

"Whoa!" Craig said, his voice full of relief. "That was close."

Chapter 2

We were up early for church the following morning. The church, the head Lutheran church in the country, had no frills. The walls were cement, painted a light blue that was years overdue to be repainted. No more than fifty seats were set up in rows, some wooden, some folding chairs. The altar was a simple table with a green table cloth draped over it. A large wooden cross hung behind it.

It had none of the gold and silver caked on the walls, the priceless artwork, the expensive grandeur I'd seen in Catholic churches across Latin America. Although I was raised Catholic, I immediately felt more comfortable in this church than I had in any cathedral I had visited in my travels. I had always silently objected to the incredible amount of money poured into beautifying churches, always felt off in churches that were more tourist attractions than houses of worship. I had always wondered if Jesus would prefer another pure gold chalice, another stained glass window, another ornate statue, or the money being used to help the people of the congregation.

It seemed like Craig knew every person in the church as we milled around waiting for the service to start, even worship being on relaxed Latino time. He greeted everyone in Spanish, and I quickly realized just how little of the language he spoke. He had warned me that his language skills were low before the trip. I didn't understand just how little he knew until I listened to him bumble his way through basic greetings and pleasantries, using no verbs in his sentences, just stringing nouns together, peppering in words in English and trying to fill in blanks with his hands as he talked.

I respected him for trying, and it was easy to tell that the people he spoke with did too. Even with my experience living and teaching in Spanish-speaking countries and the years of classes I've taken to learn the language, I remain painfully shy trying to use the language. But I've been part of no shortage of embarrassing slip-ups and faux pas to fuel my insecurity.

I had been confident in my Spanish when I first arrived in Costa Rica in 2013, my first time traveling on my own without a high school tour group and guide looking after me. After sitting on the tarmac in the Miami airport for most of the morning, waiting for a technician to arrive to fix the malfunctioning computers on our plane (he recommended turning the computers off and back on when he arrived, successfully), I arrived in San Jose, Costa Rica at twelve midnight instead of twelve noon. Thinking it was a bit late to show up at my host family's door, knowing nothing about them besides the address I had written down on a slip of paper in my bag, I elected to get a hotel room for the night. Once checked in, I wanted nothing more than to take a shower, wash the 24-hours of airports and airplanes I had just sat in off me, and go to bed.

Of course, when I opened my suitcase, I realized that my bath towel was folded up at the very bottom, underneath three months' worth of clothes, baseball gear, and supplies. After years of high school Spanish and two semesters of it in college, I felt confident that I could ask for one correctly at the front desk. I knew how to ask "May I have", I knew the word for "towel", and I knew "please".

I practiced stringing the question together a few times out loud in my room and then marched myself to the front desk. I woke the dreary-eyed late-night attendant up from his nap and asked "May I have a towel please?"

I received a blank stare in response. I repeated myself.

"A towel?" the attendant asked, disbelief in his voice.

I hadn't practiced anything else, so I repeated the question a third time. "May I have a towel please?"

"A towel. You want a towel?" He spoke slowly in Spanish, making sure I understood him. I repeated myself again.

Eventually, realizing I wasn't going (or able) to say anything else, he disappeared into a back room shaking his head. I could hear him talking to another employee.

"Gringo wants a towel!" "A towel?" "A towel!"

I heard drawers and cabinets opening and closing as they looked for my towel. A few moments later, the employee reappeared.

"Here you go," he said and handed me a tampon.

My host family was kind enough to explain the

subtle difference between the words to me the following day.

It was the first of many embarrassing language mistakes I would be a part of during my time in Costa Rica and on later trips across Central and South America.

Thankfully, not all the laughter would be at my expense. The following summer, I found myself in Ecuador, having dropped out of college to teach elementary schoolers English. At the end of the school year, I was roped into sticking around to put together an English-intensive summer camp.

When I was asked if I would like to help at the camp, the school's director forgot to mention that I would be in charge of designing and planning the entire month of activities for the students. She also forgot to inform me that on the first day of camp, after spending a sleepless weekend lesson planning four different activities for each day of camp for three different age groups for thirty days, that I would arrive bright and early Monday morning to find fifty-six bright-eyed, eager Ecuadorian children waiting to learn from me, and me alone. No other teachers had been hired.

Within the first fifteen minutes, my carefully planned curriculum was out the window, the lesson I had prepared being replaced by me frantically trying to talk the kids who had climbed onto the school's roof into coming down, while also shouting at the kids who had taken off out the front door of the school to come back, while also simultaneously and unknowingly playing a game with a group of students that seemed to be called "Tackle the Gringo".

The following days brought no improvement,

although the kids seemed to enjoy the field trip we took to the local hospital after a student who leaped from the monkey bars found out that he could not, in fact, fly. Being the excellent educator I am, I was able to turn it into a learning opportunity, and the kids went home that day knowing how to say 'broken leg' in English.

Exasperated and frustrated, I took it into my own hands to recruit help for my quickly failing camp. I knew two friends back home had been planning to travel to Latin America, hoping to learn more Spanish, and I was somehow able to talk them into changing their flight from Central America to South under the auspices that helping with my summer camp would be 'fun' and 'would look great on a resume'. Somehow, they were in Ecuador by the end of the week.

The director of the camp loved the idea of having two more native English-speakers in her school. She had decided that the declining attendance at camp was not driven by the injuries or lack of learning taking place but by a lack of marketing and advertising. Almost immediately upon their arrival, we found ourselves in the most popular public plaza in the city, handing out pamphlets for the camp, our white skin being offered as an incentive to anyone who would listen. "Learn English from real Americans!"

After our stint in the plaza, we were ushered in front of TV cameras to shoot a commercial that would air live on primetime Ecuadorian television.

The setup was simple, the Spanish easy. We were each placed in front of a table, various school supplies and an activity set up in front of each of us. We would each demonstrate a fun activity the students would do at the camp while introducing ourselves in Spanish.

My lines were simple. I would say, "Hello, my name is Daniel. Come to Summit Summer Camp and I'll teach you science!" Then I would mix the two beakers on the table in front of me, and the baking soda and vinegar inside would explode in a cloud of educational excellence.

Then the camera would pan over to my friend Jared, who would say nearly identical lines, offering to teach the students music before playing something nifty on a little keyboard in front of him.

Then Anthony would be up. He spoke almost no Spanish, but we figured after practicing repeatedly prior to the shoot and then hearing Jared and I say our lines on camera, he would be able to get through his lines without a problem.

And he came so close! I stumbled through my lines awkwardly but successfully enough. Jared was gold on the little piano. The camera zoomed in on Anthony and the table of food in front of him.

The cooking portion of the summer camp was easily the most successful part. We had picked out simple English recipes that we would teach the kids to make while peppering them with lots of useful vocabulary: food names, kitchen utensils, cooking verbs. The kids loved making a mess with the ingredients and eating what they produced and demonstrated that they actually learned something when their parents would come pick them up and demand "What's on your face?" or "What's this gunk stuck in your hair?" and they were able to tell them the name of the food, in English, that they had smeared across their body.

Anthony got through his introduction without a

hitch. "Hello, my name is Anthony," he said confidently. He picked up the knife on the table and began cutting the slab of meat on a cutting board in front of him. All he had to say was "Come to Summit Summer Camp and I'll teach your kids to cook!"

He came so close. "Hello, my name is Anthony." Big smile as he cut the meat. "Come to Summit Summer Camp." His smile got bigger as he neared the end of his line.

"And I'll cook your children!" He held up the knife, red with blood from the meat.

For some reason, attendance at camp didn't shoot up dramatically following our TV spot.

Slip-ups like these and others (like the fellow Samoa Peace Corps volunteer who had meant to tell his host mother he was sore and needed a massage and instead, by mispronouncing a word, told her he needed to masturbate) had left me shy and hesitant with my language skills. Craig, conversely, seemed to embrace his rudimentary knowledge of Spanish, laughing off every mistake and trying again.

It felt like we shook hands with every person in the church as we waited for the service to begin, Craig knowing almost every person by name.

"Personal connections and relationships make this possible," he had told me in the airport on our way, and he clearly had made no shortage of them on prior trips.

The church service began eventually, forty-five minutes late. Sergio, an athletically-built local who had picked us up at the airport the night before and would serve as our driver, translator, and savior throughout our trip, provided the music for the congregation on an acoustic guitar Craig had brought him as a gift on his last visit. I recognized the melodies of familiar church hymns but struggled to keep up with the words in Spanish.

The pastor began by pointing us out to the congregation. Necks craned and heads turned to stare down the three Gringos sitting in the back row. He then welcomed us in English to the church and the country and informed us that the service we were attending was a special one that would feature a family-oriented ceremony in which local families could come forward and be blessed. We were welcome to participate.

His homily stretched much longer than any I had heard before, and it became exhausting to continue trying to translate it in my head. I watched as the faces ahead of me also became restless as the pastor reached and surpassed the hour mark. Occasionally, he would point back to us, and I would pick up words like "charity" and "kindness" in his speech, trying to make it look like I had been paying attention as heads turned again to look at us. Communion was given eventually and the family ceremony began.

Candles were lit and placed on the floor. One-by-one, each family present walked to the front, hand-in-hand, and circled one of the candles. Some of the larger families looked like a football team huddled around their candle, their arms draped over each other's shoulders. However, there was no clap, no "break!" when they finally separated. Most left with wet eyes, some openly weeping.

Family in Nicaragua is a different concept than it is in the United States. Children don't flee home at eighteen, seeking independence. Because few can afford to attend college, most children live with their parents until they are married, and even then, many remain on the same property or move in next door. With poverty so prevalent across the country (Nicaragua is the poorest country in Latin America and the second poorest in the Western Hemisphere), especially in rural areas, survival is often an effort shared by the entire family together. Fathers and sons work long hours in fields under hot suns. Mothers and daughters mash the corn and beans the men bring home into tortillas and meals by hand and tend to gardens in their spare time to supplement their meager diets.

We were motioned to the front by the pastor when the stream of families started to slow. Not wanting to be impolite or break the sanctity of the service, we walked hesitantly to the front and formed a loose triangle around one of the candles.

"We were strangers yesterday," Craig said quietly. "And today, we're family. All thanks to baseball."

In that moment, I couldn't help but think of all the family baseball had brought me over the years. The countless teammates I had played with, still constituting the majority of my closest friends. My host family and friends I had made in Costa Rica during the adventure of a summer I had spent playing there. My families, friends, colleagues, and students in Panama, Nicaragua, Ecuador, the Galapagos Islands, Peru, and Samoa, all trips made possible by my travels playing baseball.

Following the service, the pastor headed immediately for our spot in the back row.

"Craig! Jay! Welcome back!" he said, embracing each. "Dan! Welcome!" His voice was quiet, not booming like it had been during the service, but still powerful. After a series of pleasantries, Craig began filling the pastor in on our plans for the trip. A warehouse full of baseball gear was waiting for us across town. We'd spend ten days filling the truck we had rented with gear and driving to communities until it was all given away. Then we'd end the trip in northern Nicaragua, in the driest, poorest region of the country, working to implement sustainable farming projects. We'd also be meeting with government officials and hospital owners to discuss shipping hospital equipment to Nicaragua next, a project Craig had begun by chance when a generous friend he had taken to Nicaragua to view the different projects had called him and simply said "Craig, would you like a hospital?"

The pastor thanked Craig repeatedly for his work and then turned to me. "Craig and Jay do things the right way. Most organizations who make donations to Nicaragua want their money to go to something they can see. They build a school. They dig a well. And then they leave. Everyone is willing to pay for those projects, but no one wants to pay the salaries of the people needed here to keep the schools running, the wells pumping after they leave. Of course we're grateful for their help. We need schools, and we need wells, but we're also grateful that Craig and Jay keep coming back and keep supporting the people necessary to make sure their projects are sustainable." He paused before continuing.

"And baseball. Baseball is so important here. But no one wants to give their money just so kids can play. Craig and Jay understand that baseball is more than a game here. It's hope. It's opportunity."

As he finished talking, the pastor ushered us over to the back of the church where all the families were sharing a potluck-style meal.

"Come and eat with us. You're family here."

It probably wasn't wise to ingest homemade local food on the first official day of our trip, but plates of pork rinds, tortillas, rice, and beans were thrust into our hands before we could think of a polite excuse, and the families offering stood waiting expectantly until we began putting the food in our mouth.

When we finished, we slipped out the door and to the rented truck waiting outside, Sergio having packed up his guitar and pulled our ride around. He wound us through the sign-less streets of Managua, loud Bachata pounding through the stereo system.

Our next stop was the warehouse where all of our baseball equipment was being stored. Today, we would just be taking a look, developing a plan for how we would unpack it all from the large cardboard pallets it had been shipped down in and how we would organize and then re-pack it all to distribute to local teams.

The warehouse was surrounded by tall cement walls, fifteen feet high on all sides and sprinkled with sharp pieces of broken glass on the top.

"Nicaraguan barbed wire," Sergio said with a laugh, pointing to the jagged points waiting to castrate any thief who tried to swing a leg over the wall. We had to honk to wake the guard up, sitting asleep hunched over on a bench inside the wire gate. The guard dog at his feet, a skinny mutt who had clearly recently given birth, barely looked up as we entered. Once inside the gate, we could see our warehouse, a long rectangular building built from sheet metal. Its door was flanked by thick metal chains held in place by three large padlocks.

"The most high-tech security system money can buy," Craig said, surveying the guard already asleep again on his bench, the mangy dog, the tall walls, the chains, and the padlocks.

When Sergio eventually was able to find the right key for each padlock and untangle the mess of chains on the door, we entered the warehouse. We stumbled in the dark until we found light switches dangling from small ceiling lights. They only worked on one half of the large warehouse, leaving the other half in darkness. eighteen pallets were neatly lined up and pushed against the walls on each end of the warehouse, forty feet of dusty cement floor in between.

Sergio, Craig, and Jay pose in front of the pallets of baseball gear

"It's perfect!" Craig said, turning to Sergio. He was at the lighted end, digging through one of the pallets. "Everything is exactly how I packed it. None of it has been touched. Just perfect."

He turned to Jay and me. "Tomorrow, we unpack it all. We'll have you guys start at one end, Sergio and I will take the other, and we'll meet you in the middle." He switched off the light above him. "But, that's tomorrow. Tonight, we're going to have some fun."

We returned to our truck after Sergio had re-applied the chains and padlocks to the door of the warehouse. The guard was woken from his slumber again to let us out of the gate and back onto the streets of Managua.

"Get ready for the best baseball game of your life," Craig said, excitement in his voice, as we pulled up to Dennis Martinez Stadium, the national stadium of Nicaragua named for the first and most successful Nicaraguan baseball player to reach the major leagues. Martinez, nicknamed *El Presidente* (The President) for popularity so immense in his home country that many joked he could be elected president, remains the winningest Latino pitcher in major league history with 245 wins. After twenty-three seasons in the big leagues, multiple All Star games, two World Series appearances, and a perfect game, Martinez returned to Nicaragua and opened a baseball academy that he continues to run to this day to give more young ballplayers the opportunity to succeed in baseball. Like many young Nicaraguans, Martinez grew up without access to baseball equipment, not holding a real leather baseball until he was thirteen years old.

Inside the stadium, an atmosphere existed unlike

anything I had experienced at a baseball game before. The crowd, still long before the first pitch, was on its feet stomping, clapping, and shouting soccer-style *Ole* chants. A full rock band stood on top of the first base dugout, thrashing guitars being pumped through the stadium's sound system. Flags and banners waved wildly in each section of the crowd. The ballplayers from Nicaragua and Colombia, playing in the championship game of a Pan-American tournament, hadn't appeared yet on the field, but a raucous party was already unfolding in the crowd.

"I can only imagine how loud it will be in here if Nicaragua wins!" I shouted to Jay over the noise.

It turned out that I couldn't have imagined the scene that took place when Nicaragua recorded the final out, sealing a championship victory in a tournament they had been the underdog in throughout. The ninth inning ended with a routine fly ball to center field, sealing a 12-5 victory for Nicaragua. The game was much closer than the score indicated, Nicaragua trailing late into the game until exploding for the comeback victory against a Colombian bullpen worn out from the lengthy tournament. Pandemonium broke loose throughout the stadium when the final out was recorded. As the Nicaraguan players poured out of their dugout to celebrate, their coach was doused with the obligatory water cooler bath, and, much to my surprise, so was I.

Beer was not sold in the stadium by the glass. It was sold by the bucket. Ushers roamed the aisles throughout the game lugging around pales filled with cubes of ice and a dozen cans of beer, selling the whole package instead of individual cans. After nine innings in the sun and heat, fans were left with buckets full of melted ice cubes at the end of the game, which they happily dumped on whoever was nearest them. The bucket Craig, Jay, Sergio, and I had shared throughout the game was commandeered by a fan from the row behind us and promptly emptied over my head.

We hurried toward the exit, soggy, as fans shook up any cans of beer they had left and sprayed them joyously into the air. The rock band played loudly on top of the dugout, a mosh pit of happy, drunken fans forming out of the sections behind the dugout. The stadium's only exit was behind home plate, and we quickly realized we were fighting against the current as we tried to weave our way through the chaos. We were nearly stampeded by fans streaming the opposite way towards the right field corner. The chain link fence separating the stands from the bullpen had been torn down, and fans were storming onto the field.

When we finally fought our way to the exit, the band had reversed direction, now playing to the screaming mass of players, coaches, and fans that had overtaken the field. Tonight, all the statistics didn't matter: second poorest country in the Western Hemisphere, poorest Latin American country. The only statistic of importance was the score on the manual scoreboard beyond the center field fence. For a night, Nicaragua was champion.

Chapter 3

"At the ball game last night, there were two retired numbers posted on the outfield wall," Craig stated at breakfast Monday morning. We were sitting pool-side at our hotel, a cheap but cozy little place. My room was little more than a bed, a box of a black-and-white TV, a shower that sometimes spat cold water on me and sometimes refused to leak out any water at all, and a large oil painting of a comically plump olive-skinned woman laying seductively in front of a mountain landscape in an a little too revealing red dress.

"That's a lot of woman!" Jay had exclaimed when he poked his head into my room to bid me goodnight the night before. "I'll leave you two alone."

His room had a painting of corn hanging above the bed. Clearly, I had lucked out.

"Did you recognize either of the names with their number retired?" Craig asked. I had elected to go with the traditional gallo pinto breakfast plate while Craig and Jay played it safe with eggs and toast.

My roommate for the trip

As a baseball fan, I had immediately noticed the large number 21 adorning the center field wall in the stadium, *Clemente* written above it in bold letters. Known simply as "The Great One" in Pittsburgh, Roberto Clemente, the Hall of Fame Pirates right fielder, established himself as one of the greatest baseball players in history during a career that stretched eighteen years from 1955 to 1972. Clemente amassed three thousand career hits, a lifetime .317 batting average, twelve All Star appearances, twelve consecutive Gold Glove awards, and four batting titles over the course of his career. So great on the field was Clemente that Bowie Kuhn, the Commissioner of Baseball at the time, once described him as follows: "He gave the term 'complete' a new meaning. He made the word 'superstar' seem inadequate. He had about him the touch of royalty."

More importantly, Clemente established himself as one of the greatest off the field as well as on it, renowned for his charity work throughout his career.

Following the 1972 season, one in which the 37-year-old Clemente hit .312, was chosen as an All Star and Gold Glove recipient, and notched the three-thousandth (and, tragically, final) hit of his illustrious career in his final at-bat, Clemente boarded a small passenger airplane flying from his native Puerto Rico to Nicaragua. Managua had just been hit with a devastating earthquake. Six thousand had been killed and more than two hundred thousand were left homeless.

With two-thirds of the city's residents displaced and food and water shortages exacerbating the earthquake's damage, Clemente chose to personally accompany the fourth plane-load of relief supplies he had collected to donate to the city. Dangerously overloaded with supplies, the plane never reached its destination, crashing into the ocean off the coast of Puerto Rico, killing all on board.

The following year, the Baseball Hall of Fame waived the mandatory five-year waiting period required following retirement for a player to be eligible for induction, only the second time in history it chose to do so (the first following Lou Gehrig's untimely death), and enshrined The Great One in the Hall of Fame. Every year since, the Roberto Clemente Award has been given to the ballplayer who best exemplifies the game of baseball on and off the field.

"Any time you have an opportunity to make a difference in this world and you don't, then you are wasting your time on Earth," Craig said, sipping from a small teacup-sized coffee hidden behind his massive hands, his plate empty. "Clemente said that. I doubt I'd be here today if not for his inspiration."

Our breakfast table became home to Clemente stories, tales of throws from deep right field that seemed as much legend as fact, Clemente having possessed an arm so strong that the legendary announcer Vin Scully once remarked that he could "field the ball in New York and throw out a guy in Pennsylvania". Craig recalled watching Clemente catch a ball on the warning track in the right field corner of the spacious Forbes Field and the runner on second simply standing on the bag, tipping his helmet to Clemente, knowing he'd be thrown out if he tried to tag up.

Eventually, our conversation drifted from Clemente to the other number retired in Nicaragua's national stadium.

"Nemesio. Number 14," Craig told me when I tried unsuccessfully to recall the name. "So great he's known only by his first name."

I would search the internet for statistics for the player Craig called the greatest in Nicaragua's history when I returned to my hotel room that night and find his name splashed across the record books. His accolades included the best career batting average in Nicaragua's history (.354), and his name was at or near the top of Nicaragua's career leaders in nearly every offensive category: first in runs scored, first in doubles, second in walks, third in hits, fifth in home runs, and an unbelievable .439 batting average during the 1992 season.

"He's Babe Ruth here. And then some. Not only is he the greatest player in the country's history, but he is now the president of the country's baseball federation and has made it possible for countless youth here to play the game. Without his help, we would have never gotten our container of gear through the government. We'll be meeting with him this afternoon to say thanks and discuss where all the equipment will end up."

"It's like landing in the United States and having Derek Jeter and Bud Selig meet with you. That's how big Nemesio is here," Jay added.

We would meet Nemesio in the afternoon. Our morning would be devoted to meeting with the bishop of Nicaragua's Lutheran church. Much like Nemesio, she had played an instrumental role in helping us get the baseball container to Nicaragua, allowing us to use the church's name to gain tax-exempt status for our equipment. Previous groups that had tried to do similar work in Nicaragua had discontinued their donations to the country after being met with significant tax bills at the border.

Following the two meetings, the rest of our day would be spent unloading the pallets in the warehouse, organizing the equipment, and loading our pickup truck to begin distributing the gear across the country on Tuesday.

We began back at the church we had attended service at the previous day. Listening to Craig talk about his projects was entertainment in itself. Cramped into a small back office at the church, the bishop, much younger than I expected her to be, sitting across from us in street clothes, Craig wandered the room, too excited to sit while explaining all of the latest work the non-profit was partaking in. He talked as much with his hands as his words, filling up the room with his booming, gravel-scraping voice and gesticulations. Even though Sergio was there to translate, he still peppered his sentences with words in both Spanish and English.

When Craig speaks, his stories digress and regress. What could be accomplished in a few sentences takes five minutes, but you're held spellbound the whole time. Simply explaining how the hospital project started took fifteen minutes. Craig wound the story through present and past, telling an anecdote from Tel Aviv in the '70s, a story of the Nicaraguan Revolutionary War in the '80s, stopping quickly in Mexico right after he graduated college, before somehow arriving back at his current goal to bring hospital equipment to Managua. It all made sense when he got there, eventually.

The conversation went back and forth through Sergio. Both sides were very grateful and appreciative of the other for their help. The health of everyone's family members was discussed. Our flight was good. Yes, we did enjoy the church service yesterday. Eventually the conversation became more businesslike. Dollars and cents were discussed. The church had picked up many of the unforeseen expenses of shipping and transporting the container, and Craig was adamant about reimbursing them for their money, time, and labor.

As I listened to the bishop describe the amount of work the church had taken on to help us, I couldn't help but wonder why a church would be so invested in a baseball project. The paperwork alone had been extensive. Transporting the container the equipment was shipped in from the coast back to Managua had required a semi-truck. Unloading the pallets into the warehouse took heavy machinery and manpower. Why would the church devote its meager resources to getting kids a few baseball bats and gloves, especially from a secular non-profit?

When there was a lull in the conversation, I asked, not expecting to receive an answer as lengthy or insightful as I did.

"Hope," the bishop began, pausing to think. Although I understood the word in Spanish, Sergio translated it for me. "With unemployment, poverty, drugs, and so many other problems here, the youth don't have any hope. Baseball is hope."

Her voice filled with conviction as she continued. "The youth here have so much responsibility in the rural areas at such young ages. The children here grow up too fast. There's no opportunity for them to get an education or to simply be children when they are worried about helping put food on the table for their family. With no education and no opportunity, it's easy to fall into alcohol and drugs."

She paused to let Sergio translate and to let me write.

"So many organizations won't give money so kids can 'play'." She emphasized the words with her fingers as she said them. "Baseball is more than playing. When kids are playing with a stick and a bunched up pair of socks and you give them equipment and uniforms, they believe that there is hope for them in the game. They see the Nicaraguans who have made it in baseball, and they think they could be next. Going to practice, going to games, being on the team gives them a reason to stay away from drugs and alcohol."

She turned to Craig and Jay and addressed them directly.

"When people in the United States donate money

to Nicaragua, it rarely gets here. Money the church gets promised for projects can take months or even years to arrive, if it ever gets here at all. It often gets divided up and sent to projects in other countries or disappears somewhere in the government. We start projects to help people and then never receive the money promised to finish them. You actually come here, bring the money and equipment yourself, and make sure it gets where it needs to go. We cannot thank you enough for that."

By now, I was writing up the side of my notebook page, trying not to miss a word.

"For Nicaraguans, it's so much more than just being given money. It's about seeing the faces, knowing there are actually people who care about them. Kids wear the uniforms you bring proudly because it has the logo of a team back in the United States who cares about them enough to donate. It unifies communities in ways that cash does not. Obviously, money matters and does good, but having people like you who care enough to actually come to Nicaragua makes a longer-lasting impression on the people here."

The room fell silent for a few moments as her words sunk in for each one of us. I had been skeptical coming into the trip about what kind of impact we would actually make in people's lives by simply bringing them baseball gear. Would a couple bats and a couple balls actually make any difference for anybody here?

Watching Craig's face, I could tell that the bishop's words were vindicating for him. I'm sure he had been asked the same question over and over again, and I'm sure he had wrestled with it himself. In a country with so many problems, heck, in a world with so many problems, should he really be devoting his time and money and his donors' time and money to baseball equipment?

"You probably won't believe this," the bishop picked up after the pause. "But church attendance increases and stays up for a month after you visit Nicaragua. That's hope."

With that, the bishop shook each of our hands in turn, thanked us again, and offered her help in any way that we might need while in Nicaragua.

We left the church silently, digesting the bishop's words, and rode across town to meet with Nemesio. His office was in, what can only be called, a high-security gas station. An armed guard stood outside the main door, a towering metal gate that took a comically oversized key to unlock.

"Nemesio bought into the gas station business when he retired. He's as good of a businessman as he was a ballplayer," Craig told me quietly as the guard let us inside. "Also," he whispered. "Don't go asking him any big questions like you did the bishop."

Once the guard let us inside the main door, we were met by another uniformed member of Nemesio's security team. Through another locked door, we found ourselves in a small office lobby. A well-dressed secretary offered us drinks as we were seated in chairs lined up in front of an ornate bookcase. Pictures of Nicaraguan ballplayers hung in frames on the wall. I recognized Cheslor Cuthbert, the young Royals infielder, and J.C. Ramirez, a Mariners relief pitcher. Managua was still buzzing about Cuthbert, who had recently returned to Nicaragua fresh off a World Series championship and played an exhibition series with the local professional team, selling out the stadium every game. Only twelve Nicaraguans have ever played in the Major Leagues, and to have Cuthbert return home, not just a big leaguer but a champion, had ignited national pride and passion for the game.

We waited in silence, the armed guard standing just inside the door, watching us. A poster of Nemesio was tucked in the corner, propped on top of a filing cabinet. *Nemesio Porras: The Unforgettable Legend* the headline in Spanish on the top read. Nemesio was pictured mid-swing, at the point of contact with the ball. Nicaragua was splashed across the front of his uniform in bold blue lettering on top of his famous number 14. I worked to translate the rest of the cursive script but was interrupted by a line of men entering the room.

We were quickly engulfed in a line of handshakes and introductions. I was so busy trying to decide which of the six men who had entered the room was the baseball legend that I almost didn't catch the name of the stout, heavily-goateed man shaking my hand.

"Hey, I'm Marvin Benard. Nice to meet you." His English had just the faintest hint of an accent.

The baseball fan inside me went crazy.

"*The* Marvin Benard?" I asked instead of introducing myself.

"I don't get that reaction very often anymore," he said with a chuckle.

I've been half-heartedly teased most of my life for knowing more about baseball than any self-respecting young man should (and whole-heartedly teased for a host of other things). In college, I was banned from playing 'the name game' on the bus to ballgames, a popular time killer on long, boring rides, because of my acumen for remembering the most trivial and obscure baseball players in the game's history. The rules were basic. One person would call out the name of a baseball player, and the next guy in line would have to name a player whose first name started with the same letter as the last name of the previous player (That was a mouthful. Example: Joe **M**auer, **M**anny Ramirez). If you couldn't name a player that fit the criteria, you were eliminated. If you threw out a player whose first name and last name started with the same letter (**M**ark **M**cGwire), the order would be reversed (making former Tigers closer and current attempted murderer Ugueth Urbina the ultimate trump name).

A typical game would go like this:

"Bryce Harper." "Harmon Killebrew." "Kris Bryant." "Barry Bonds. Reverse!" "Brad Radke."

A game against me would go like this:

"Albert Pujols." "Porfirio Altamirano." "What? No. You made that name up." "Relief pitcher in the '80s. Nice mustache, too." "Fine. Adam Wainwright." "Wonderful Terrific Monds III." "Shut up." "No, really! Braves prospect in the '90s. Never made it to the bigs though." "That doesn't count then!" "Fine, Wladimir Balentien." "Who?" "Oh, come on. He played in the majors. Plus, he set Japan's single season home run record!" "This isn't fun."

Marvin Benard's name was one that stood out to me because he had been in the right place at the right time. He was the center fielder and leadoff hitter for the Giants on October 5th, 2001, the game in which Barry Bonds set the single season home run record with his 71st and 72nd long ball of the season, a game I had watched with rapt attention as a 9-year-old and then on repeat on tape for weeks after. The 1998 home run chase between Sammy Sosa and Mark McGwire had ignited my love for baseball as a kid, and Bonds' pursuit of the record just three years later had cemented it. In the following years, I would rip the posters of those sluggers off my wall as curse words like "steroids" and "performance enhancing drugs" and "the cream and the clear" scarred seemingly every headline about the game. Thankfully, my love for baseball was one of the only things that escaped the era untainted.

Looking back, it's ironic that home runs made me fall in love with baseball as a kid, since it was home runs (more so, my penchant to give them up) that would push me out of the game years later as a pitcher in college.

Now, to say that I remembered Marvin Benard simply because of his association with Bonds' record would mean marginalizing a very solid 9-year career with the Giants. In his prime, Benard was a rare combination of speed, strong outfield defense, and left-handed power that provided both extra base hits and home runs from the top of the lineup. Following his retirement, the Giants honored Benard's career by inducting him into their Wall of Fame, and he still leads all Nicaraguan-born players in every offensive category at the major league level.

None of the six men who had entered were Nemesio. They milled around the room, talking quietly in Spanish. Benard chatted with us in English. He had recently been named the manager of Nicaragua's national team and was preparing for the upcoming World Baseball Classic qualifiers. He listened politely while Craig explained the non-profit's work.

When Nemesio did appear in the door, guard in tow, it was easy to tell he was the legendary ballplayer before any introductions were given. He had an air about him that filled up the room, that made all conversation stop as soon as he entered. A loose-fitting dress shirt hung off his athletic frame, the top two buttons undone, a silver chain necklace hanging in their place. He shook our hands and introduced himself amicably before sitting down and folding his hands.

"What do we need to talk about today?" The question wasn't unfriendly, just businesslike. Craig explained the latest news for the non-profit again, the container filled with donated gear, the warehouse we would be unpacking later that day, our plan to distribute it around the country in our rented pickup truck. He thanked Nemesio for his help getting the gear into the country and through customs.

The meeting was quickly over. Nemesio offered to help in any way he could and to provide contact information for more teams that could use gear if we ended up having leftover equipment after our planned stops. After more handshakes, we were led back outside to the gas station's parking lot. It was late afternoon by then, and traffic had picked up.

Sergio swerved our truck through downtown Managua. Like many countries I had traveled to, Nicaragua seemed to lack even the most basic rules of the road. Stop signs served as little more than roadside decorations. Right of way didn't seem to exist. Cars pulled out whenever they felt it should be their turn and gestured angrily at any car that disagreed. Drivers turned left at stoplights from the farthest right lane, weaving between lanes of traffic coming from both directions. Street performers, salesmen, and window washers added to the chaos by standing in intersections at red lights trying to make a living. Even within the city, traffic was often slowed by horse-drawn carts and livestock marching down the streets.

The guard was napping again when we pulled up to the warehouse gates. Sergio pounded the truck's horn, startling the man awake. He stumbled over to unlock the gate, one hand rubbing sleep from his eyes. The guard dog barely looked up as we drove in.

"The best security money can buy!" Craig said cheerfully, more amused than sarcastic. Sergio wrestled with the chains and padlocks on the warehouse door.

Once inside, we flipped on the working light. The cement floor was covered with a layer of dirt that kicked up when you simply walked through, making the entire room appear hazy in the dim light. Eighteen pallets were lined up at each end pushed together so tightly that there wasn't space to squeeze between. On top of each pallet sat a large cardboard box, extending to chest-height, filled to overflowing with baseball gear.

We attempted to sweep the floor with a flat piece of cardboard, simply hoping to clear enough dirt out of the way to make room to stack equipment, but we quickly found ourselves choking on dust.

"Well, Dan and Jay on one side, Sergio and me on the other?" Craig suggested. We separated. We designated areas in the middle for each type of equipment. As we unloaded the first few pallets, neat, organized piles of gear formed on the warehouse floor. Bats were separated by size, full-sized baseball bats in one pile, youth bats in another, softball bats in a third.

Uniforms were laid out by team and color, sets donated by colleges and high schools from all over the Midwest forming a rainbow of cloth down the middle of the warehouse. First basemen's mitts were stacked in a pile, catcher's gloves next to them. The rest of the gloves were sorted by size and hand.

Outside, the afternoon sun pounded down aggressively. In the warehouse, the sheet metal walls trapped the heat, exaggerating it, making the air heavy and hot. The work was not easy. The pallets had been packed haphazardly, different types of equipment shoved into every empty space to maximize the amount that could fit into the container. Each box was a menagerie of bats, balls, jerseys, pants, gloves, hats, catcher's gear, spikes and miscellaneous baseball items like batting tees and bases. Over the course of the afternoon, we each logged miles of walking back and forth across the hot, dirty warehouse, arms full of equipment each way.

The boxes were deep enough that we were unable to reach the items at the bottom, and I found myself climbing in and out of them, handing armloads of gear to Jay before climbing back out and helping him sort and distribute it. The dirt in the air, kicked up by the movement in the warehouse, clung to the sweat on my arms and face, forming a layer of slimy mud on my skin.

As the sun set outside, our neat, organized piles disappeared under mounds of baseball gear.

(Next page: our warehouse at different stages of the unpacking process)

"Where do shin guards go?" Craig shouted across the warehouse, arms full of catcher's gear.

"I've been putting them on top of the first base mitts," Jay shouted back.

"I thought that's where the baseball pants were going?" I asked from inside a box.

"No, no. Baseball pants go under the softball bats!"

By the time darkness settled in outside, we were, quite literally, wading through piles of baseball equipment. The stack of batting helmets was shoulder high and volatile. Each of us found ourselves buried by an avalanche of helmets after bumping the pile trying to climb past it. The dirty floor had completely disappeared, and there was hardly a foot of warehouse left you could walk on without stepping on plastic or leather or aluminum. More than once, I fell with arms full of gear after stepping on a loose baseball and having it roll out from beneath me. Thankfully, there wasn't anywhere to fall without landing on soft leather gloves or cloth uniforms.

When Craig showed me the inventory list in the airport—over six thousand balls, eight hundred gloves, fourteen hundred bats, seven hundred helmets, and thousands of jerseys—I hadn't been able to comprehend just how ridiculous of an amount of baseball equipment that was. Standing back, looking in the warehouse from outside, as Craig happily tossed the last armload of gear into our mess of equipment, raising his arms above his head in celebration, it was almost overwhelming to see.

Craig had worked for over a year collecting the equipment, driving across six states to pick up donations from schools, universities, and teams.

Individual donors had chipped in, grandmothers whose grandsons outgrew their glove and bat, parents who found a few dirty balls in their garage after their kid went off to college. Craig hadn't just collected all the gear, he'd helped pack it all, all thirty-six pallets. Both he and Jay, in their sixties, could be relaxing at home in retirement, but instead they choose to work late into the night in oppressive heat, doing hard physical labor in a sauna of a warehouse thousands of miles from home.

"I'm too old for this crap," I joked when Craig joined me outside, the night air still impossibly warm, trying to make light of my youth. He laughed, hands on his hips, trying to catch his breath. He poured water from a gallon jug into his mouth and then over his head.

"Tomorrow, it'll be worth it," he said. "Tomorrow we get to meet our first teams. You'll see why Jay and I are here."

With that, he set his water down and headed back into the warehouse, his break over. He grabbed an empty duffle bag from a pile near the door and began packing for our first stops the following day. I shook my head, amazed at both his energy and passion, and followed him back inside.

Chapter 4

"Welcome to the most dangerous neighborhood in Nicaragua!" The man shook our hands, introducing himself as Denis Martinez, the catcher, not the pitcher. "And welcome to the Academia Mimadas Rubilena Rojas, Nicaragua's only softball academy!"

Behind Denis stood a line of young, athletic women, each in a blue and white uniform with the academy's logo across the chest. Jay winked at me and nodded towards the girls. I had told them over breakfast that I was single, but hadn't elaborated on the mess that is my love life (I use the present tense there because I'm sure, whenever you read this, it will still be a mess).

We had originally pulled up in our truck, bags of softball equipment in the back, at one of the saddest ball diamonds I had ever seen. The entire field was dry dirt. No baselines or batter's boxes were chalked. Instead of bases, someone had simply sprayed white spray paint in a heap in the general area where bases should have been. A wooden board had been dropped where the pitching rubber would have resided. The outfield had no fence.

One girl wearing a jersey with number 15 across the back sat in the cement bleachers behind home plate. Besides her, the field was completely empty.

"You sure this is the right place?" Craig asked Sergio, looking around the empty field. Prior to the trip to Nicaragua, Craig had asked him to try to find softball teams in Nicaragua to donate to. It had proved a challenging task. Women were not typically allowed to participate in athletics in the country, strict gender roles relegating them to domestic activities. Sergio had been tipped to this field by a friend of a friend who thought he had seen a team of girls playing on it, the best tip we had received in Managua.

Helping Kids Round First was officially formed by Craig in 2009. The efforts of the non-profit were grassroots at first, simply Craig carrying suitcases of baseball gear with him on flights to Nicaragua and giving it out when he arrived. However, his link to Nicaragua far preceded the non-profit. In 1984, he traveled to Nicaragua with a group of Americans to support the leftist Sandinista movement in their fight against an oppressive dictatorship and to protest human rights violations against rural Nicaraguans.

While there, Craig's group traveled through dangerous active war zones, volunteering to help rural communities by picking cotton in their fields, working and living with local families to ensure their health and safety while the war raged around them. When word got around that Craig was a talented pitcher, a baseball game was scheduled between the American volunteers and local Nicaraguans, armed soldiers bordering the field to protect the ballplayers. The local community they played in had just one ball and one bat. When Craig returned to the United States, he helped arrange for new baseball equipment to be delivered to the community.

Three decades later, he was still helping Nicaragua and still looking to enact change. After years of bringing baseball equipment to the country, wondering how he could help women gain more opportunity, he had decided to add a stipulation to all of his baseball donations. Any team that accepted a donation of baseball gear would also receive an equal amount of softball gear which they would have to find a local softball team to give to or start one in their community.

"There's going to be push back," Craig warned me in the airport during our planning session. "There will be men who disagree with women playing sports. But baseball is going to help us cause change."

The difference in opportunity between men and women in Nicaraguan sports was glaringly evident when we entered the softball academy, the girl who had been waiting at the field sitting in the bed of our pickup shouting directions to Sergio through an open window. On my first trip to Nicaragua, as a player, we had the opportunity to play at and tour Dennis Martinez's (the pitcher) baseball academy in the city of Rivas. The academy featured a spacious, well-kept field with bullpen mounds down each foul line and a batting cage beyond the right field fence. A large dormitory housed all of the players with classrooms and a mess hall attached. The academy had no shortage of equipment, buckets of balls were scattered around the field as were bags of bats. Each player had their own name brand glove and was outfitted in a full uniform and metal spikes.

The same could not be said about the softball academy. We were given the full tour, Denis and a female instructor leading, the girls trailing behind, waiting to jump in to demonstrate the different drills and equipment they used for practice. The academy was housed in a warehouse building much like the one we had rented to store our equipment. About fifty feet of spotty green turf lined the floor inside. Surrounding it, mismatching netting was hung and tied together to form a batting cage.

Denis showed off the academy with pride. The girls had recently won the Central American Women's Softball Championship, a six-team tournament featuring teams from Belize, Costa Rica, El Salvador, Guatemala, and Panama, despite their lack of equipment and facilities.

"Most of the girls that come here are very poor. Some are homeless. We do our best to provide for them with the resources we have." He pointed into a closet-sized room with cement walls. Three cots filled the room. "Some of the girls sleep here at night. We find room if others need a bed."

We stepped into the room to look one at a time. With the cots taking up almost all of the floor space, there simply wasn't room to fit multiple people in the room at once.

"The biggest problem we have is girls coming here hungry. You can't train, practice, or get better if you haven't eaten. We do our best to have food available, even if it's not much." We poked our heads into an equally small kitchen. Two girls in uniform sat next to a metal pot set over an open flame. A mixture of rice, beans, and chicken simmered inside. "The girls take turns cooking for each other."

We were led next to the far side of the batting cage. Metal posts with a spider web of bungie cords hanging from it held a softball in place at waist height.

"Most of our equipment is homemade. This one I made myself. The cords make the ball come right back in place so you can hit again." The girl in the number 15 jersey who had met us at the field stepped up to demonstrate. The grey bat in her hands was visibly dented, and any logos that had adorned it were long worn off. "Since we don't have very much equipment, we focus on using proper technique and mechanics."

Number 15 walked us through an elaborate routine before swinging the bat. First, she held the bat up flat across her shoulders, showing that the length of the bat from the end of the barrel to the grip on the handle was as long as her shoulders were wide. Then she laid the bat down across the home plate on the floor, the end of the bat touching the far front corner of the plate. She marked with her foot where the end of the bat rested, then turned the bat ninety degrees so the barrel pointed behind home plate. She lined her back foot up with the end of the bat and then her other shoulder width away.

"That's how we line up every time we hit to make sure we have the right size bat and are standing in the right place. We learned that from Crystl Bustos."

Bustos, a two-time gold medalist cleanup hitter for Team USA softball, had visited the academy with Venezuelan softball star Ruby Rojas (for whom the academy was named), instructing the players on all facets of the game. The girl then swung for us in slow motion, breaking down the parts of a proper swing,

Denis narrating the whole process. She took a few ferocious full-speed swings, making contact with the ball with a satisfying crack, the entire contraption shaking from the force.

We were led outside where the academy's top pitcher was getting warm. The bullpen was nothing more than a strip of sidewalk with netting set up at the end to stop wild pitches from escaping. A mannequin with a batting helmet on its head was propped up near where the catcher sat in oversized catcher's gear. The pitcher stood balanced on a two-by-four that was propped up so it angled down towards home plate.

"This helps with balance and mechanics. If you don't use proper technique, you'll fall off." The girl went through her motion, throwing a strike and landing gracefully on the board. Had I ever been required to pitch on a balance beam, I would have ended up in the hospital.

The bullpen at the softball academy

We were shown the academy's lone batting tee next and another contraption Denis had made.

"This lets four girls practice at once, since we don't have very much space." He had taken a piece of orange pipe about five feet tall and pounded it into the ground. At the top, four smaller pipes stuck out horizontally like helicopter blades. A thick strip of leather hung from each. He instructed four girls to demonstrate how it was used. They lined up surrounding the machine, each facing one of the strips of leather. In unison, they swung. The strips of leather spun around the pipe after they made contact.

"The one that spins the longest is the winner," Denis told us as the girls prepared to swing again. "Behind, you can see our weight room." He gestured beyond his contraption. I tried to see what he was pointing to but only saw a pile of boulders stacked against the fence surrounding the academy.

"We have rocks of all different weights. It's not much, but it works. We have one more batting machine back by the weight room. I made it by hanging a scuba diving fin from a post. It works well for teaching the girls to swing through the ball."

As the only softball academy in Nicaragua, this was the best of the best available to women in the country.

"Facilities and equipment have been a big challenge for them," Ruby Rojas told me about the academy named in her honor. She had visited first with US Olympian Jessica Mendoza on a trip sponsored by the US State Department to help empower women and girls through sports around the world and made subsequent return trips to Nicaragua on her own to continue supporting softball in the country. Despite the humbleness of their academy, Rojas was impressed by the girls' passion for the game during her visits.

"I was really touched by how much the girls there wanted to learn. It did my heart good to see them embracing the sport the way they did."

Rojas works globally to help empower women and sees great value in using sports as a tool to pursue that goal.

"Girls can turn to softball to give them a reprieve from what they're facing away from the field. The relationships they make, the lessons they learn, and the importance of teamwork and unity they experience will carry over to help them in many facets of their life. It gives them hope, which you can't put a price tag on."

We held a small ceremony in the bullpen, the girls crowded in, some sitting on plastic chairs, others standing. Craig talked briefly about the non-profit before focusing on his mission to help give women more opportunity in sports in Nicaragua. He lauded the girls for their dedication to the game despite the adversity, opposition, and poverty they faced each day. Jay and I were pulled up front to present the top hitter and top pitcher from the academy with brand new Spalding gloves.

Denis followed by thanking us profusely for our visit. While he spoke, we were presented with heaping plates of rice, beans, chicken, and tortillas. Only after we had finished eating were we allowed to present the equipment we had brought for the academy. We had six duffle bags full, complete with bats, helmets, catcher's gear, shorts, game pants, uniforms, dozens of softballs, and a new glove for each girl. During the ceremony, the girls had formed a polite semi-circle facing Craig, Jay, and me. When we started unpacking the gear, they crowded around us, eager to see their new equipment. I began handing gloves to the girls surrounding me. Every time I handed another glove from the bag, a chorus of thank yous rained on me in both English and Spanish. The girls' ages varied widely, from early teens to early twenties, and they distributed the gloves to their teammates according to size.

Soon the small bullpen area became hazardous as the girls swung new bats, broke in their new gloves playing catch, hit balls off new batting tees, and tested new catching gear. I pulled Denis aside, eager to hear more about the academy and the impact the donated equipment would have.

"This is a very dangerous neighborhood," he told me. "There is a lot of crime, a lot of drugs, and a lot of abuse here. Without softball, many of these girls would be on the streets. Some were homeless, some were addicted to drugs, most were in broken homes when they came here. Some already have children of their own." He gestured towards a small toddler running back and forth between the girls, a batting helmet bouncing up and down as she ran, a glove on each of her hands.

"Here, they can have different lives. They have food here. They have a place to sleep here. For many, this is their home, and this is their family. Scholarships are available through sports, so softball gives them an opportunity for an education and a career they could not afford otherwise. We are able to meet their basic needs here and give them the chance to do more with their lives.

"We train the girls physically here to be better athletes and better softball players. But we also focus on training them mentally. Women are not respected here, especially in this neighborhood. Abuse against women is common. We work hard to improve their self-esteem and their confidence. We want to..." Sergio, who had been translating the conversation for me, paused.

"I'm not sure how to say that word in English." He pulled out his phone to translate the word. "Empower. They want to empower women in this neighborhood."

"Softball gives hope to other girls in the neighborhood as well," Denis continued. "Seeing our girls in the stadium, playing just like the men, gives women pride. Young girls in the neighborhood know that there will be opportunity for them to play, to come to the academy, to have a home and a family someday. It's an incentive for them to stay away from the crime and the drugs that are easy to fall into here.

"It truly is a miracle that you found us today." He had been watching the girls play with their new equipment while he spoke, but he turned now to look me in the eyes. "You see the equipment we have. It is not much. The equipment you brought us today will keep this academy running. When I was younger, I traveled to the United States. I got to watch softball and baseball practices there. I will never forget how much equipment they had. The outfielders had a bucket of balls to take fly balls with. The infielders had a bucket of balls to practice fielding with. The pitchers had their own bucket of balls. The hitters had a bucket of balls. The catchers had a bucket of balls. They had enough bats for everyone to be hitting at once. All the different positions could practice at the same time. Here at the academy, we have one bucket of balls and just a few bats. Only one or two girls can be practicing at a time. This is the first time anyone has donated to our academy, and now we will be able to actually practice."

We shook hands. I found Craig standing in the middle of the chaos, talking with a few of the players. A look of relief came over his face when he saw Sergio was available to translate and his broken Spanish could be given a rest.

"Sergio, could you tell them that we will be back here in the future with more gear and ask what kinds of equipment they need most?" Sergio relayed the question to the girls. They conferred for a few moments before answering.

"We always need more softballs. And shoes, if it's possible. Normally we share shoes for our games." I hadn't noticed prior, but most of the girls were in sandals. Only a few were wearing tennis shoes. "And we don't have any batting gloves. And..."

She tailed off. The other girls started giggling.

"And we need softball underwear." Bright red had crept into her cheeks.

"Well, we have lots more softballs and some batting gloves in the warehouse," Craig told them. "We'll make sure some get to you. We should be able to get shoes to you on a future trip. As for the softball underwear, I'll buy some sliding shorts new for you ladies. Don't think you would want those to be used." We all laughed as the girls thanked Craig.

After taking a series of pictures—some formal, all of us lined up in front of the piles of equipment, some silly, each of us wearing a batting helmet and holding bats and gloves in the air—we bid the academy farewell and returned to the truck.

The softball players with Craig, Jay, and myself

Craig was almost giddy with excitement, talking nonstop as soon as we had pulled away.

"Sergio, I could kiss you right now!"

"Please don't."

"Thank you for finding that academy for us. What a perfect place for us to donate to. Seeing a place like that makes me think that it will be possible to get girls more involved here in Nicaragua." He turned to face Jay and me in the back seat. "That was incredible, wasn't it? Now, this next stop is incredibly important, too. Without the support of the health ministry, we will never get a hospital into this country."

Sergio, proving to be invaluable to our trip already

as a driver, translator, and contact with local teams, had found a way to set up a meeting with the leaders of Nicaragua's health department. He had gotten wind that the different departments of the country's government played against each other each year in an ultra-competitive men's softball league. Our plan was to inundate them with softball equipment and then slip in a plug for the hospital project, hoping that they would be receptive to helping us down the road.

"I really dislike the idea of giving donated equipment to adults with well-paying government jobs. But, if they're willing to help us with the hospital because of it, it will be worth it. The last charity that tried to ship a baseball container down here stopped coming to Nicaragua after receiving a twenty-thousand dollar tax bill. Can you imagine how much the taxes would be on expensive high-tech hospital machines?"

We pulled up to the Department of Health's complex, a series of pristine white buildings with MINSA (short for Ministerio de Salud) stamped on the side in red lettering. Soldiers in camouflage army uniforms stood on either side of the towering, barred gate. Sergio conferred with them out the driver's window, explaining that we had a meeting scheduled.

Once inside, duffle bags of softball gear in hand, we were led to a small meeting room. Two long tables sat parallel to each other across the middle of the room. Government officials in matching white polo shirts with the MINSA logo on the breast shook our hands before sitting down at the table across from us. Handmade posters on the wall listed information about communicable diseases around the world: HIV, malaria, ebola, chikungunya. The poster labeled Zika was blank. The mosquito-borne illness was in the process of causing worldwide panic, and clearly Nicaragua was no closer to finding a cure than any other country.

The government workers sat expectantly at their table in silence. Sergio nudged Craig.

"They're waiting for you to talk." Beyond the handshakes when we entered, there had been no pleasantries. These men were all business. Craig rose and began pacing between the two tables, unsure where to start. He hadn't expected to get the opportunity to give a full pitch.

He greeted the ministry employees and introduced Sergio, Craig, and myself. The men nodded to each of us in acknowledgment, faces blank.

He gave the same spiel about the non-profit's baseball work, efforts to increase opportunities for women, and farming projects that I had gotten used to hearing already. When he began talking about hospitals, his demeanor changed. His words became less jovial, heavier. He talked about touring hospitals in Nicaragua. Patients were on cots in the hallways, all the rooms filled. The medical equipment was outdated and rudimentary. The rooms were dirty, the patients uncomfortable. After touring just one hospital, the friend he was touring with was pale in the face and asked Craig if they could cancel the other tours they had scheduled.

"I've seen enough," he pleaded, stricken. A few weeks later, he called Craig and simply asked, "Would you like a hospital for Nicaragua?" Craig was taken aback. He hadn't planned to expand the non-profit into health, but knowing how many lives could be improved and saved with high-quality medical equipment, he said yes.

He told the health department workers about the equipment waiting in his warehouse in South Dakota: electric hospital beds, ultrasound machines, X-Ray devices, fetal heart monitors. He talked about Luis, a local taxi driver who he often hired to drive him around Nicaragua on his baseball trips. They had visited Luis' mother in the hospital after she underwent brain surgery. She was crowded into a small room with eight other patients. The room was not air conditioned, the heat almost unbearable. She passed away shortly after their visit from complications from the surgery, the poor hospital conditions no doubt playing a role.

It wasn't hard for me to picture what the hospitals must be like in Nicaragua. While teaching in Ecuador, I opened a two-inch gash on my forehead after fainting from dehydration while sick with food poisoning. My host family rushed me to the only clinic open in the middle of the night, where I was put on to a rock hard cot next to a man bleeding profusely from a cut on his leg. The doctor sat between us, alternating between stitching my forehead and sewing up the man's leg, using the same tools on both of us, not pausing to wash or sanitize them.

The government workers did little but nod as Craig spoke. What he was saying was not news to them. However, when we started pulling equipment out of our bags and laying it before them, the demeanor in the room changed. The men, important government officials all at least in their forties and fifties, were children on Christmas morning. They tried on batting helmets, pounding on each other's and laughing.

Uniform tops were pulled over their dress shirts, good-natured arguments breaking out over uniform numbers. A portly man in glasses strutted back and forth in full catcher's gear, pounding on his chest like he was King Kong. Softballs whizzed through the air in the small meeting hall as new gloves were tested.

"What do you think?" Craig asked, gesturing to the gear but probably hoping for an answer on the hospital projects.

"Everything is great," came the response from the man who had sat at the center of the table during the meeting, now pounding a fist into a new black outfielder's mitt. "Except the bats. They are for children."

Craig and Jay turned to look at me, eyebrows raised. I had been assigned to pick out and pack the bats for the visit the previous night while the others handled the uniforms, gloves, balls, and helmets. I had chosen the longest bats in the warehouse, assuming they were for adults, not paying attention to their weight. During a meeting as important to the future of the non-profit as this, I had given the government workers Little League bats.

"That's what you get for letting a pitcher handle the bats?" I said. The concern on Craig's face loosened, and he cracked a smile as Sergio explained my joke to the workers.

"We'll get you some new, heavier bats this week. And we won't let the pitcher pick them out this time!" Craig told them.

"Thank you for everything. A new glove costs hundreds here. A bat costs three hundred or more. To the average Nicaraguan, that's months' worth of paychecks. We're the smallest department of the government and often don't have the resources to get any equipment for our team. We used to borrow from the other departments, but after we won the championship last year they stopped being so kind. We have a game Saturday morning, and it would be an honor to us if you would come."

"We'll be there, with new bats," Craig said. They shook hands, and we lined up to take pictures. Before any were taken, a massive three-tiered trophy was pulled into the room.

"Thanks to your help, we will win another trophy this season!"

As we packed up to leave, shaking hands goodbye, we were pulled aside by one of the eldest workers. "Thank you again. When you need help, you will get it from us." Craig beamed as he shook his hand. A hospital would be coming to Nicaragua.

After spending a few sweaty hours in the warehouse packing for the next day's deliveries, we sat beside the hotel pool, beers in hand, and reflected on the day.

"That was one of the best days of my life." Craig said, his voice a mixture of sincerity and disbelief. It could have been hyperbole, but knowing Craig and his passion for his work, I didn't doubt him.

Chapter 5

I woke up tired but excited. Coming from
Minnesota in the middle of the winter, the Nicaraguan
heat felt oppressive. Every night the thin blanket the
hotel provided ended up on the floor next to the clothes
I had tried to wear to bed.

It was a welcome change, being kept up at night by
the heat and not my own thoughts. Back home, it had
been weeks since I had slept an entire night through, the
breakup haunting me. I should have realized then that
my sadness went past what was normal following a
breakup: the lack of sleep, having to make a conscious
effort to force myself to eat even my favorite foods, the
complete absence of motivation, drive, or interest I felt
each day, the way I clammed up completely and
absolutely in anything that bordered on a social
situation. It was exhausting to simply get myself to
whisper a 'yes' or 'no' answer to my own parents.
Getting myself out of bed was a challenge each
morning, as if gravity had been doubled just for me.

Hell, there were days when I was teaching that I

would close and lock my door during my prep period and sob in my room, only wiping my eyes and pulling myself together when the students would start knocking on my door.

So, despite the heat and the lack of sleep, simply being excited in the morning for the upcoming day was refreshing. I had good reason to be excited. For the first time, we would be leaving the capital city of Managua and it's relative wealth and traveling to more rural parts of Nicaragua.

Sergio had lined up ten teams for us to meet and donate to. We had packed duffle bag after duffle bag the night before, making sure we would have enough gear for every child who showed up. After filling the bed of our pickup truck and strapping an unsteady pile of bags to the roof, we still had a stack of bags sitting on the warehouse floor. Craig called Luis, the local taxi driver, Orvin, an English-speaking real estate agent who owned an SUV, and Jonathan, a friend of Orvin's who had his own truck. Even with four vehicles, we still had to shove gear inside each car, resigning ourselves to the fact that we would most likely each have to wear batting helmets and sit with bags of equipment in our laps simply to fit inside during our drive across the country.

Not only would we be leaving Managua for the first time and meeting young ballplayers in numerous communities, we would be heading south, ending our day in San Juan del Sur, the same city I had visited on my first trip to Nicaragua three years prior. Jay's one requirement for each trip was to get to spend an afternoon surfing, and we had designated this afternoon to be his. I had first learned to surf in San Juan del Sur.

Although every time I had tried since I had stumbled to shore bruised and battered, choking on salt water, my complete lack of ability to actually surf never dampened my enthusiasm for trying.

Of course, the last time I had tried, my students on the Galapagos Islands dragging me out to the ocean after class, I lost my swim trunks to a particularly powerful wave. Nothing helps you bond with your students like washing up on shore pantsless. I'd make sure to tie my trunks as tight as I could this time.

Despite San Juan del Sur being an exceedingly beautiful city with a pristine beach buffered by high bluffs, the statue of Jesus looking over the bay, my intentions were not all good. I was ready to track down and finally get my revenge on that damn monkey.

Jay and I squeezed into the backseat of the truck, trying to delicately balance the stack of batting helmets piled between us so they wouldn't topple over into our laps. The morning sun had barely risen, but it was already impressively hot.

As Sergio drove us out of Managua, the other three vehicles in our caravan following, the scenery quickly changed from city to wasteland. The country vegetation was dull in color, the persistent drought that had made farming nearly impossible in the region draining all of the life from the plants. The open plains were bone dry, the ground cracked from the relentless sun. Dead brown leaves hung from sad trees spotting the side of the road.

We passed through small communities of cement houses, the paint on the outside faded and peeling. Ox carts shared the highway with us. Herds of livestock were driven down the side of the road by farmers searching for a pasture with surviving grass in it.

Everything out the window—the houses, the trees, the fields, the people—looked as if they needed a fresh coat of paint.

Craig and Jay had made numerous trips to Nicaragua together over the years, spending hundreds of hours driving across the country to deliver donations. To add novelty to each trip and break the monotony of long hours in the car, they selected a band each trip and listened to their complete discography while traveling. Previous trips had featured the Grateful Dead, Bob Dylan, and Bruce Springsteen.

Jay had been left in charge of the music on this trip and chose a folk band called Tallgrass. He pulled an ancient MP3 player from his bag and hooked it to a small portable speaker.

"I heard these guys play live a few weeks ago." Acoustic guitar accentuated by quiet banjo filled the car. "They're like bluegrass slash folk."

Simply hearing the description, I expected to hate the music. But, I found my head bouncing to the slow beat as I gazed out the window. The song blended the line between folk music and alternative rock. The singer's voice was husky and forlorn, Citizen Cope with added country.

The music, melancholy and western, complemented the rural scenery I watched roll past out the window. The dried grass, the bare trees, the whining banjo, it all fit together like Jack Johnson songs at the beach.

Our first stop of the day was at a small daycare in the community of Belen. After visiting on a previous trip and finding that the daycare's entire library was in Italian, donated by a European tourist, Jay had made it a personal project to collect children's books in Spanish and English to donate on each trip. It was his suitcase of books that had saved us from a full customs inspection at the airport.

Delivering the children's books to the Belen daycare

The daycare was housed in a colorful orange and yellow single-story building. Inside, art projects covered the walls. The daycare was run by two young mothers who were able to provide for the thirty-five children who came daily on meager government funding and donations.

We were given a tour of the small facility while the owners explained their purpose to us. The daycare had two main open rooms, littered with toys. A small kitchen was lined with stacks of boxes with the logo of Feed My Starving Children stamped on the side. During high school, I had spent an afternoon scooping cups of rice into dry-seal bags for the charity, wondering if it would actually ever feed starving children. Standing in the cramped kitchen of the Nicaraguan daycare, a few of the children who attended lingering outside the door gawking at the tall, lanky Gringo inside, I felt pride well inside me knowing our efforts were making an impact.

"Most women are unable to work in Nicaragua. They are expected to stay home with the children. Our daycare makes it possible for the women of Belen to have jobs. They aren't glorious jobs—textiles, cooking, cleaning, sewing—but it allows them to have a career and earn extra money for their family," we were told as the tour concluded back at the main gate.

Our caravan was soon back on the road after the tour. The first field we arrived at was in downtown Belen. A rusty metal grandstand held up cement bleachers behind home plate. Crunchy, brown grass carpeted the infield, blending in with the dirt. The field had no bases. A horse wandered in left field searching for grass worth eating.

Thirteen young ballplayers waited for us on the bleachers. Their coach, Johnny Alvarez, had met us at a nearby gas station to provide directions to the field. In a country with no street signs or addresses, gas stations were one of the only easy to find landmarks and meeting places. Johnny had served as the pitching coach at Dennis Martinez's baseball academy for many years, working with many of the top prospects to come out of Nicaragua. Just recently, he had chosen to start his own academy, aiming to train younger prospects than Martinez's academy would take. The ballplayers on the field in front of us, some as young as seven, others in their early teens, were some of his handpicked prospects.

As he would at every stop, Craig spoke with the players for a few minutes to begin our visit, explaining the goal of Helping Kids Round First and telling the names and locations of the different universities, high schools, amateur teams, and sponsors they were receiving gear from. The kids did their best to listen politely, but their eyes continually wandered to the piles of bats, balls, gloves, helmets, catcher's gear, and uniforms spread out on the ground in front of them.

We outfitted each player in a donated red and black mesh uniform with 'Mavericks' scrawled across the front in block letters. On some of the youngest players, the jerseys hung down below their knees, but the size did nothing to dampen their excitement. They had arrived wearing mismatching uniforms in all different colors. Now their team had matching uniforms, regardless of whether they had any idea what the name on the front meant or not.

They tried on new spikes, trying to find a pair that fit better than their uniforms. Some were successful. Others clomped back and forth in shoes that made them look more like clowns than ballplayers. We watched for a few minutes while the kids played with their new equipment, all smiles, before heading back to our vehicles. We had nine more teams to meet and only so much day to do it, especially if we were going to get to San Juan del Sur to surf.

There was a game going on at the second field we pulled up to. As soon as our trucks were spotted behind home plate, the players began sprinting off the field. The pitcher, too focused to notice, delivered a pitch home, not knowing there was no defense behind him.

The players vaulted the short chain link fence surrounding the field and were crowded around our truck before we had even unbuckled our seat belts. The eldest of them couldn't have been older than ten. Some wore t-shirts and shorts, some were in jeans, others were in full uniforms. They were a rainbow of different colors: three in baby blue jerseys, four in orange, two in yellow, one in navy, a few in whites and tans and greys. One wore a New York Yankees jersey, and I silently decided he'd be last in line to receive equipment.

Craig spoke and then we presented the gear. When we packed up to leave, every kid was in new white baseball pants and a red University of Nebraska-Omaha jersey. They paraded back to the field with arms full of new gear to resume their game. They were already playing again when we drove away.

The third field had no fence and had more horses on the infield than players.

"You asked me to find you softball teams," Johnny said as we climbed out of the truck. "It wasn't easy, but here's one of them."

Instead of handshakes, the twelve girls hugged Craig when Johnny introduced him. Craig spoke shortly, lauding them for pursuing opportunity in sports and affirming his dedication to empowering women in Nicaragua. With no coach to speak on their behalf, the girls thanked us directly.

"We could not have played this year without your help. All of our equipment is borrowed from the boys nearby. If they have a game on the same day as us, we have to forfeit." The girl speaking reached into the pink backpack she wore and pulled out a navy blue ball cap.

An Oakland Athletics style cursive A decorated the front. "This year, the boys will come to us to borrow our equipment!"

She presented the cap to Craig, explaining the A stood for Amazonas, their team name.

"It's not much, but we want you to have it so you can remember the Amazonas, the team that would not have played this season without your help."

Craig fitted the hat onto his head while the girls clapped. He wouldn't take it off again the rest of the trip. We tried to get the girls to pose for a group photo, but most were already playing catch with new gloves.

"I stopped buying souvenirs when I travel decades ago," Craig told us in the truck as we headed for our next stop. "I don't have any room left for them, and I just give away anything I bring home anyways. But this hat, I'm keeping this forever."

Craig (far right) trying on his new Amazonas hat

Stops four and five were more of the same. Young baseball teams, short speeches, handshakes, distribution, smiles, pictures, goodbye. We met our sixth and seventh teams in a dusty clearing.

"Where is the field you play on?" I asked one of the players, a young boy in a floppy ball cap.

"This is our field!" I looked at the space in front of us. There were no bases, no dugouts, no fences, no mound. I could barely tell what direction the field faced. Left field was a large hill lined with trees. Small prickly shrubs grew out of the infield dirt.

We met our final team of the day in the late afternoon. Not knowing we would be meeting each team individually instead of at one central meeting place, we had told them we would arrive at ten in the morning. It was now past four in the afternoon. We found an entire team of softball players waiting still at the field when we arrived.

'Field' is an incredibly literal term in this case. The girls' ball diamond was a farmer's pasture. It was a funny change. At every other field we had visited that day, we found livestock grazing in the outfield, the ball fields being the largest patches of grass farmers could find. Now, we found the reverse, ballplayers playing on farm land.

Even after waiting six hours for us, the girls were incredibly gracious and grateful. They told us it was the first time they had received any equipment before. For years, they had watched the boys teams in the area be gifted gear on numerous occasions, but no donor had ever paid attention to them

"That's my goal," Craig told them. "To give girls the same opportunities as boys here."

We left with all four vehicles empty, having given away hundreds of bats, gloves, spikes, uniforms, helmets, and balls. Tallgrass pumped through Jay's speaker as we raced the sun down the highway trying to get to San Juan del Sur while it was still light enough to surf.

We barely made it, Sergio speeding through downtown and then down a bumpy dirt road to get us to the beach as the sun started to fade behind the horizon. Jay and I rented surf boards and were in the water just in time to watch the sun disappear. After a few hard falls, I was content to just let the waves rock me back and forth as stars came out above me, trying to think of anywhere in the world I would rather be.

Chapter 6

I was incredulous when I looked up "How many Nicaraguans have played in the major leagues?" on the internet and found the answer to only be twelve. How could a country so devoted to baseball not have more success getting players to the game's highest level?

As we drove across Nicaragua, baseball was everywhere. Not just at the fields we visited, but in front yards, pastures, even in the streets, kids playing in the road using a stick and taped up pair of socks, dodging traffic. Baseball jerseys were as common of attire as t-shirts. The constant presence of baseball everywhere we went made the fervor for soccer I had seen in South America seem weak by comparison.

During my first trip to Nicaragua as a player, we had watched Kevin Gadea, a lanky teenage right-hander who threw mid-90s fastballs past our team of college ballplayers, sign with the Seattle Mariners and had figured it was a common occurrence.

I called Nick Holmes, a Major League scout who had been assigned to Nicaragua by the Texas Rangers during my first visit to the country, to try to find out how Nicaragua had slipped through the cracks as a baseball hot spot despite their passion for the sport.

"There has been an increase in interest in Nicaragua in recent years, but it has been slow. When I first began scouting there in 2011, less than a third of the league had a scouting presence there. Now, nearly every Major League team sends scouts to Nicaragua."

Nick and I had tried to connect multiple times since I had returned from Central America three years ago. Every time he called, his phone number had a different country code in front of it. Although still scouting, he had formed his own business, World Baseball Experience, leading tours for baseball players around the world while also bringing home the stories, experiences, struggles, and successes of international prospects trying to make it to the big leagues.

"There is talent in Nicaragua, even if it is not as well-developed as it is in countries like Cuba, the Dominican, or Venezuela. Teams are competing against each other to find talent, and since every team has an academy and coaches and scouts in those big countries, they're looking for the next untapped source of talent. Once a few teams were successful in Nicaragua, the rest followed."

Entering Spring Training 2016, five active Nicaraguans had Major League experience. Although that number is small, especially since two of those players were free agents entering camp, it is the greatest number of players Nicaragua has had in the majors at one time.

"Nicaraguans still face a hard road in baseball. Although all teams scout here now, no Major League team has established an academy here to train prospects like they have in other Latin American countries. It's part of the reason the Dominican has hundreds of players signed each year while Nicaragua has just a few. They lack the instruction, the coaching, and the development that other countries have. There are baseball academies in Nicaragua, but many have closed in recent years. Those that are still running are taking fewer players. It's incredibly expensive to house, train, feed, and educate young ballplayers, and the academies only get paid if the player gets signed."

For the players themselves, getting signed is just the beginning of a long, arduous path that often ends far short of the Major Leagues. Most players signed out of Nicaragua leave the country poorly educated and struggle to adapt to life in the United States. Although the academies that train them are also supposed to provide schooling for the players, the academies receive no money for good test scores, only for results on the baseball field, and education is rarely prioritized.

"For the players, education is one of the biggest roadblocks they face. They come to the United States and they can't speak English, they can't ask for anything they need, they can't do simple math, they're the only Nicaraguan in a clubhouse often segregated by home country, and they have no idea what their coaches are saying to them. The coaches don't care. They have a job to do and need results, so it's figure it out or you're gone. The signing bonuses Nicaraguans get are minuscule, and the teams don't have very much invested in them. So, if they aren't able to understand instruction and get better, they're on their way back to Nicaragua."

Bob Oettinger, the president of the International Baseball Association, an organization with close ties to Nicaragua, echoed Holmes' sentiments.

"Most Nicaraguan players do not speak English, and many have limited education and have never been given nutritional or conditioning regiments. Most have also never had money and are victimized by unscrupulous agents. I've heard stories from Nicaraguan players who have played minor league ball in the United States who were so unprepared and intimidated that they wouldn't leave their hotel rooms when not playing and would order the same food every day because they didn't know enough English to order anything else."

Roniel Raudes is one of those players who has struggled to adjust to life in the United States. Growing up in Nicaragua, he rarely had equipment to play baseball with beyond a glove and pair of shoes his dad gave him. Signed at age sixteen by the Boston Red Sox, Raudes went first to the Dominican Summer League, a common spot for Nicaraguan prospects to be sent to train under the tutelage of Major League coaches in the much more developed baseball academies of the Dominican Republic. He excelled there, striking out sixty-three batters while only walking three in over fifty innings of work. After only eleven games in the Dominican League, he was called up to the Gulf Coast League Red Sox, Boston's Rookie League affiliate in the United States. After going 3-0 with a 0.90 ERA in four starts, he found himself on the mound for the Red Sox in the Gulf Coast League championship. Although he was one of the youngest players on the field at just seventeen, Raudes threw five shutout innings, striking out seven batters, and picking up the win in the deciding game of the championship series.

"It was a great experience," Raudes says about the game. "Before the game, I prayed and asked God to help me. I told Him this game is for my family and for my people, the people of Nicaragua."

Although he has been very successful on the baseball field, life off of it has been challenging.

"I had to leave my family behind. It's hard. It's something that hurts every day that I am in the United States. The majority of the year I am in the United States. I go seven months without seeing them."

Raudes spends much of his time off the baseball field studying English and trying to continue his education.

"The truth is, it is very hard knowing almost no English. I am working very hard trying to learn new words every day."

Houston Astros catching prospect Marlon Avea has struggled with many of the same things Raudes has since leaving Nicaragua in 2011. A veteran of five seasons in the minor leagues, Avea has been forced to adjust to being away from his family.

"You just get used to it. It's not easy, but you get accustomed after being away this long," he told me when I asked about his family's impact on his career. While he has been able to adjust to the distance between him and his family, English has remained a problem for Avea since his debut in the United States in 2014 following three seasons in the Dominican.

"It is a real pain not knowing the language," he said as we discussed his catching statistics. I had asked him about his tremendous defensive numbers behind the plate, and he admitted that he had no idea what his statistics were. He had tried to look them up before on the internet but wasn't able to understand the English abbreviations and titles on his own player profile.

We opened up his statistics on Minor League Baseball's website together.

"Which of all these numbers is my percentage for catching runners?" he asked. Looking at the page, I realized just how confusing it would look to someone who doesn't speak English. There were nineteen different statistical categories on the screen, each marked with an abbreviated title. Rows and rows of numbers appeared underneath. We translated them together, adding up how many runners had tried to steal off of him and how many he had thrown out, finding that he had a tremendous 58% caught-stealing rate in 2015.

"I didn't know that I had a good percentage," he remarked when we finished. To baseball players, their personal statistics are sacred. Most batters have already calculated their new batting average before they get back to the dugout after an at-bat. Heck, I still know exactly how many innings I pitched, batters I struck out, and what my earned run average was my senior year of high school six years ago off the top of my head (I know the same numbers for my college career as well, but I've worked hard to forget those). I could only imagine how frustrating it must have been for Avea, playing at the professional level where your next paycheck depends solely on your performance on the field, to not know enough English to be able to find out how he was doing. I asked him about it, and he responded with a laugh and a slang Spanish phrase that translated loosely to 'it's a real pain in the ass'.

Holmes hopes that the increased attention Nicaraguan baseball has received in recent years due to more scouts traveling to the country and the success of players like Cheslor Cuthbert and Erasmo Ramirez in the major leagues will help create more opportunities for players and help alleviate some of the roadblocks that players face both at home and in the United States. Continued success from prospects like Raudes and Avea would go a long way.

"If more Nicaraguans make it to the big leagues, there will be more interest and effort from both sides."

Marvin Benard, Nicaragua's most successful position player in the major leagues, agrees with Holmes.

"People get excited," he said about Nicaraguan players making it to the majors. "It fills kids with the sense and hope that that could be them someday because there is living, breathing proof that it is possible."

Even with recent successes, Oettinger estimates that Nicaragua is twenty years behind other baseball countries in terms of resources and development.

"The country suffered from the effects of the revolution years ago. At that time, most American companies pulled out, and many affluent Nicaraguans moved to the United States. As a result, they don't have the industry or infrastructure that exists in other countries. Baseball was also decentralized, and each town ran its own program."

Despite the lag in development in Nicaragua, the recent attention it has been given by major league scouts and teams is promising for the future of the country. Although no major league team has established an academy in Nicaragua, the MLB recently started a branch of their Amateur Prospect League in the country. The league gives top young prospects the chance to compete against each other in front of American scouts. The MLB has also established a permanent office in Managua and holds showcases for top Nicaraguan ballplayers in front of pro scouts.

"I think Nicaragua is now being seen as a more viable place to do business, and there is a growing number of training programs for baseball players. Our view has been that Nicaraguan can become a mini version of the Dominican Republic, although its population is much smaller. Baseball is the national game, and there is a national pride and enthusiasm for the game. We have seen the talent, but it needs to be developed."

Oettinger is hoping to play a part in that development through the International Baseball Association.

"Our short-term goal has been to identify players who have the potential to play pro or college ball in the United States and establish a training program for them, utilizing our resources with former MLB players in evaluating talent, and setting up training programs which can be implemented by Nicaraguan coaches. The long-term goal is to build an academy in Nicaragua."

His project has been plagued by challenges. Getting baseball equipment to the players has proved difficult. The Nicaraguan government impounded an entire container of gear they tried to ship to the country.

Troubles finding acceptable fields, passable roads, electricity, internet, and sponsors have slowed the project's growth. However, he has not wavered from his vision of helping to provide baseball players the opportunity to succeed in the game, complementing baseball instruction with cultural and life-training skills necessary for them to succeed in the United States.

Much like Oettinger, Johnny Alvarez is hoping to provide more opportunity for Nicaraguan ballplayers from within the country. After his own baseball career that brought him to the United States to play for Lewis and Clarke College, an NAIA powerhouse that won two National Championships during his playing career there, he spent six years training pitchers at Dennis Martinez's academy. Five of his pitchers were signed by major league teams.

After leaving his job as pitching coach at Dennis Martinez's academy, he has worked to establish his own baseball foundation to train young prospects. His dream is to teach kids about the game of baseball and help improve their lives and their family's lives by helping them sign with professional teams.

Like many Latin American countries, Nicaraguan baseball is run by *buscones*, 'searcher' in Spanish, combination baseball coach/agents who train, house, and feed top prospects and then sell their services to the highest bidder. Buscones typically keep a large portion of a prospect's signing bonus and first contract as well as a cut of their future earnings in baseball. In countries like Cuba, where players routinely receive six- and seven-figure signing bonuses, business with buscones can become incredibly dangerous. In Nicaragua, where much smaller signing bonuses are common, the element of danger is thankfully absent. However, buscones still receive a hefty portion of their players' salaries, leaving little for the players and their families.

"When I was young, a lot of people helped me become a baseball player. Without my coaches, I would have never learned the game of baseball. Now, I just want to give something back to the kids in my town. I want to try to help them sign major league contracts without taking any of the money from them once they sign."

As altruistic as Johnny's vision is, it has proven a hard project to get off the ground. Craig has been instrumental, outfitting Johnny's players with equipment and uniforms, but with no income being generated through his players' success, finding enough money to pay his coaches and keep food on the table for his own family has been tough.

"I want to help improve these kids' lives, but it takes money and resources. Our country is very poor, so we need as much help as we can get."

Hopefully, with the increased attention Major League Baseball has given Nicaragua in recent years, that help will be on the way, giving more Nicaraguan ballplayers the opportunity to experience signing a contract with a major league team, a moment Raudes remembers fondly.

"My dream came true. I couldn't sleep for days after signing with the Red Sox. I was so excited."

It could take many years for Nicaragua to reach the same status as other major Latin American countries in baseball, but with continued investment in the country it is not an unreachable goal. When asked if Nicaragua could catch up with other global baseball powerhouses, Avea didn't pause to think before responding.

"Si se puede."

Yes we can.

Chapter 7

We didn't get back to our hotel in Managua until well after ten PM following our long day of deliveries and surfing. We would be back in the truck at six-thirty the following morning to pack for the long ride to Somotillo, a city in the hottest, driest, poorest, and northernmost region of the country. I knew my alarm would come quick and I could feel the exhaustion in my bones, but I knew I had no chance at sleeping. The day deserved to be reflected on.

So, I turned the shuffle on my iPod on and laid in my bed, the ridiculous painting of the plump, seductive woman hanging over me, and tried to make sense of the day.

We had brought baseball equipment and opportunity to hundreds of young boys and girls in one day. During our initial meeting with the bishop, she told me, "It doesn't matter if it's just one ball and just one bat, the people here are so excited." It hadn't been just one ball and one bat. Each team had received fifteen bats, fifty balls, two complete sets of catcher's gear, a glove for each player, uniforms, pants, hats, and spikes.

I had wondered going in if we would actually be making a difference just giving kids new toys to play with. After meeting the players, after seeing the rundown fields they played on and the basic equipment they played with, after seeing the excitement on their faces and the glimmer of hope in their eyes, I knew we had done something good. It was unlikely that any of them would ever escape the poverty of Nicaragua, but their childhoods would be better because of baseball. Even if the odds were stacked high against them, with proper equipment they would have a chance.

For me, regardless of how minor my impact may have actually been, knowing I had been part of giving kids hope was uplifting. As my depression had pulled me down in previous weeks, I had often felt the pull of hopelessness. To know that I had helped deliver hope to others, however small, let a small bit of it sneak back inside me.

I could feel my eyelids start to be pulled down when a line from the song quietly coming through my earphones woke me back up. "I'm half the man of the men who drive me places." It was Ben Rector, one of my favorites, singing softly over a piano. Sergio had just put in a twelve hour day in the ninety-five degree heat, carrying heavy bags of equipment, driving late into the night while we slept in our seats, translating, bargaining, locating teams, setting up meetings, doing all the behind the scenes work that made our projects possible.

Yet when we visited the communities and the teams, all of the ceremonies, the applause, the thank yous, the gifts, the photos were for Craig, Jay, and myself while Sergio stood off to the side holding the camera. Without him, without Luis, Orvin, and Jonathan, without the bishop and all the Nicaraguans making our work possible, there would be no Helping Kids Round First.

"And now everything's not given, I work hard to make a living, but I'll give credit where I think credit's due. Maybe you got dealt a good hand, maybe you play it the best you can, but I don't know how far you'd walk without those cards in Howard and Danny's working shoes," the song went. The names of the men who drove us places were different, but the message was the same. "But that's just the way it goes, you're dealt a good hand and you get celebrated. Oh, how am I the only one who knows, I'm half the man of the men who drive me places?" I put the song on repeat and drifted to sleep.

My iPod had run out of batteries by the time my alarm went off. I threw on the same pair of shorts I had worn the previous two days and one of my endless supply of baseball jersey t-shirts and wandered out of my hotel room rubbing my eyes.

Craig was already sitting at one of the small poolside tables. Papers were spread haphazardly on the tabletop in front of him. He hadn't shaved in days, and his eyes were red and lined by dark bags. Frankly, he looked like hell.

"I didn't sleep much last night." I could tell. "Sergio and I had a heart-to-heart last night about the direction of the non-profit, and I've been up all night planning." I sat down across from him and tried to make sense of his notes. They were a mess of lines and half-finished, scribbled thoughts.

"Sometimes I wonder if my work here matters, and

I asked Sergio what we can do better to help Nicaragua more."

Craig quit his job to devote himself to his non-profit work. Even though yesterday had been a testament to the value of his work, his insecurities, fueled by his desire to truly change lives, still sometimes surfaced.

"He told me that we're doing good things, but we're doing a lot of things. He recommended I focus on one thing and develop a plan going forward."

The advice had reason. With baseball, farming, and hospitals as major projects and smaller projects like the books for the Belen daycare, Craig was likely stretching himself thin. As the non-profit continues to grow, could he possibly manage and coordinate all of the projects himself?

As true as Sergio's words might have been, I could tell they didn't sit well with Craig. The crumpled papers on the floor next to him confirmed my suspicion.

"Is any of this possible if I stick to just one thing?" He was asking himself more than me. "If I was only here for baseball, I would have turned down an entire hospital for Nicaragua. If I had stuck to the plan of just being a baseball charity, there would be no farming projects, no medical work, no books."

Even though he protested vocally, the bags under his eyes and the pages of notes in front of him proved he had taken Sergio's words to heart. I left him with his thoughts, not aiming to be pulled into his existential crisis at six in the morning.

We were at the warehouse by seven and were packing equipment until ten. Even early in the morning, the temperature was creeping towards ninety. I was on jersey duty all morning, sorting piles of clothes by team, color, and size and stuffing matching sets into bags for the children of Somotillo. Something told me I had been assigned jersey duty due to the inability to pack the correct bats I had demonstrated a few days earlier.

It was Thursday already, our fifth full day of the trip. The ride would be a long one, up north within miles of the Honduran border, and the forecast called for the temperature to rise even more the farther north we went.

I was asleep in the backseat of the truck before we left Managua. My rest was fitful, the constant swerving of the truck through traffic and the persistent honking of horns making it hard to stay asleep for long. I kept trying and eventually dozed off completely as the traffic thinned out on our way out of the city. I had always had an impressive ability to fall asleep as soon as I sat down in a vehicle. Back when I was still playing ball, it didn't matter if the trip was a few hours or the ten minute bus ride to our high school's rival neighbor town, I would be out before we left the parking lot and wouldn't wake until a teammate jarred me awake upon arrival.

During my first year of college baseball, I was curled up in my seat at the front of the bus (Veteran players got the back of the bus. I was an 'FNG' at the time, a life form lower than scum on a college baseball team. The 'N' and 'G' stand for 'New Guy', and you can probably figure out what the 'F' stands for) on a road trip to a doubleheader. Our pitching coach went looking for me, wanting to talk about the scouting report since I was scheduled to pitch out of the bullpen. He walked right past me, hat pulled over my eyes, slouched down in my seat against the window.

"Has anyone seen Venn?" he asked my teammates. The older guys saw their opportunity and ran with it.

"Venn? No? You mean he's not up front with the other FNGs? Oh, shit! We forgot Venn!"

A teammate woke me up and let me in on the joke. I hid under my seat when the pitching coach came back to the front of the bus, trying not to laugh as he explained to the head coach that he had forgotten to count heads before we left campus and a player had been left behind.

When we arrived at our opponent's field, the older players called the coaches to the back of the bus and distracted them while I snuck off giggling. When the team walked into the dugout, I was sitting on the bench, sadness spread all over my face.

"You guys forgot me!"

I had been a valuable part of the pitching staff all season, both as a starter and reliever. As our doubleheader wore on, I remained on the bench while two freshmen who hadn't appeared in a game yet that year got my innings.

After the games, our coach called me aside in the dugout.

"We needed you today," he told me sternly. "But you sleeping on the bus and then pulling pranks showed me you didn't come prepared to play today." I didn't throw an inning the rest of the season.

I was bitter about it for years until Steven, my longtime roommate and one of the freshmen who debuted in that doubleheader in my place, confided in me in our apartment during our senior season, "I was going to quit baseball if I didn't get in to a game by the end of the year. Thanks for taking a nap!"

It's funny how things have a way of working out sometimes.

When I woke up in Somotillo, the air was a dry and painful ninety-five degrees. It looked like we had driven into a sepia filter. Nothing grew in the heat, and the locals couldn't recall the last time it had rained. Everything, the people included, seemed to be coated with the brick red dust that stretched as far as you could see.

Craig had been stopping in Somotillo for years with baseball gear and farming projects. He was engulfed in hugs and shouts of "Señor Craig!" as soon as he climbed out of the truck. It was easy to see the poverty in the region just looking at the people: dirt smeared across ripped clothes, soleless shoes, bare feet. But, seeing Craig and our caravan of donated baseball gear, authentic smiles broke out across their faces.

As recently as 2010, the World Bank estimated that nearly half of Nicaragua's population lives on less than $1 a day, and over three quarters of the country lives on less than $2 daily. The majority of that poverty is concentrated in the mountainous, desert-like northern region of the country that houses Somotillo. The men and women before us heartily greeting Craig were mainly subsistence farmers. They worked the dry fields surrounding Somotillo, often for no pay, simply hoping to bring home enough food at night to feed their families.

Here, baseball held a deeper meaning than it did in the cities of central Nicaragua. There, it was a ticket out of Nicaragua, a chance at a signing bonus and a flight to the United States. Here, the kids knew that no scout would ever wander so far away from civilization, past where light poles and paved roads stopped. Baseball was a distraction. It was a way to forget for a few hours the mud brick house and paltry meal you would be going home to in the evening. It was a way for children who rarely finished elementary school, their labor being needed at home instead, to play and experience something that resembled a childhood.

Thirty or forty kids of all different ages waited for us at a dirt ball field. Most were boys, but a team of ten female teenage softball players was mixed in.

"Thank you so much," the girls told us, stepping forward to shake our hands hard when we approached. "We have no equipment, only the spirit. We've been waiting for your visit so we can start playing."

Somotillo's softball team

The normal pomp and circumstance followed as we presented the gear. We listened to speeches from coaches, shook hands, and took photos. I wandered off while Craig spoke to the group of players. The youngest kids had already snuck off to start a pickup game on the dusty field.

I joined them and was treated to the purest game of baseball I had ever seen. Not a single blade of grass grew on the field. Home plate was carved out of wood and tossed in the dirt. There was no pitching mound, and the bases were t-shirts dropped in the general vicinity of where bases should have been.

The two teams shared one bat. At the end of each inning, the batter who made the third out would lay the bat next to home plate for the other team to use before taking his spot in the field. Each fielder would set his glove in the dirt at his position after the third out, the teams only having nine gloves in total. The catcher had an old strap-on mask, an oversized chest protector, and no shin guards. Only a few wore baseball pants. Most were in shorts with a few in faded blue jeans. The game would stop frequently as both teams searched for their only baseball hit foul into the brush surrounding the field.

Despite their lack of equipment, despite their lack of an actual baseball field, the players demonstrated impressive athleticism and understanding of the game. The oldest player on the field couldn't have been older than ten, yet I watched a batter lay down a perfect sacrifice bunt to move up a runner. A shortstop in jeans started a 6-4-3 double play, the second baseman vaulting a sliding runner to complete the play. Bob

Oettinger had told me that Nicaragua was a fertile area for talent and I was watching it play in front of me.

A pitch is delivered home on Somotillo's dirt field

I was pulled away from the game by shouting behind me. The ten female softball players were arguing loudly with the male coaches of the little league players gathered. A pile of equipment sat between them. Craig was trying to moderate the rapid-fire Spanish disagreement to no avail.

"What's going on?" I asked Sergio, who was watching with an amused look on his face.

"The men want to take all the gear with them. They say they'll divide it and make sure all the teams get the same amount later."

"What are the chances they actually give any to the girls?"

"None. That's why they're arguing. The girls are refusing to leave today unless they have their equipment in their hands."

Craig was hopeless in the middle of it.

"I should probably do something, but it's fun to watch. Women here never stand up to men like this."

The temperature had crept over one hundred degrees, but the argument was hotter than that. Sergio relieved Craig in the middle of the shouting. Within minutes, the men had stormed off angrily and the girls were picking out the equipment they wanted from the piles.

"That's empowerment on some scale!" Craig said joyfully, knowing a new team of girls would have the opportunity to play.

We bid farewell to Somotillo shortly after, promising to return the following week to visit the farming projects in the area. On our way out of town, we stopped at Gypsy's roadside store. Gypsy was a longtime friend of Craig and Jay's. At just twenty years of age, she had organized a team for the women in her community despite significant backlash from the men in the area. She had spent years selling food to travelers out of her homemade wooden stand, using the money she earned to support her softball team.

Word had traveled quickly that we were in the area, and a crowd was waiting for us when we arrived. After we greeted Gypsy, who was barely five feet tall and looked even younger than her age, we were introduced to the crowd, all men from nearby baseball teams hoping to go home with new equipment. As Craig explained our work, the crowd grew. Soon traffic was held up by the gathering surrounding the roadside stand hoping to get a glimpse of the Gringos with the free baseball gear.

We grouped the ballplayers together for a photo, me standing in the middle of the road with my camera to catch the scene, annoyed motorists honking at me. As Gypsy's team tried to find space for themselves in the photo next to all the men, one of the male ballplayers shouted, "Get on your knees....where you belong!" in Spanish. The men laughed at the lewd joke and high-fived the one that had made it.

A few minutes later, when Gypsy's team left with all the gear, the men were no longer laughing.

We made a short stop in the city of Chinandega before heading back to Managua. This far north, the majority of the houses out the window were either made from mud bricks or were just stacks of sheet metal nailed together. We passed over bridges that once extended over rivers. With the ongoing drought reaching years in length, the river banks were dry and cracked. Only trickles of water had escaped the heat. Locals still sat on the dry river bed trying to bathe or wash clothes in the muck that remained.

Baseball was everywhere I looked. Fathers and sons played catch in front of their homes. Pickup games far short of full teams played in pastures next to cows. Kids hit rocks they picked up off the street with sticks. In many ways, northern Nicaragua was hell. But for baseball at its purest, it was heaven.

Chapter 8

Craig and Jay talked the entire trip back to Managua, reminiscing about prior trips and adventures. They had been friends since high school and had seen much more of the world together than just Nicaragua. Their banter made staying awake on the long ride home worthwhile.

Simply listening to them interact, regardless of how grand their stories were, was worth the price of admission alone. They were a testament to the theory about opposites attracting. Jay, quiet, acutely aware of the people around him, speaking slowly and haltingly like he needed to carefully consider each word before he said it. Craig, boisterous, cocksure, bulldozing through sentences as quickly as he could think them up. Jay was the mouse, Craig the lion, from the old nursery fable.

Their conversation spanned the 1970s and '80s, eventually winding to Jay's first trip to Nicaragua with the non-profit. One moment had stuck out vividly to him on his first trip, spurring him to keep coming back for years. Driving in the same region of northern Nicaragua, on their way to an equipment drop in

Somotillo or Chinandega much like we had just made, their truck had passed a small pasture where a few young kids were shooing away cattle to try and play a game of baseball. They held a ball made from taped up socks and had pulled a stick from a nearby tree to hit it with.

"I told our driver to stop and got a bat and ball from the back of the truck and brought it to them. I couldn't communicate with them at all, but their smiles and repeated graciases spoke more than words would have."

"You really can't speak any Spanish. Remember when you bought that horse?" Craig jumped in, laughing in anticipation of the story.

Jay's head fell in faux embarrassment. He tried to start telling the story, but couldn't control his own laughter. Craig handled it instead.

"Get this, Dan. We were at the farming projects, and one of the farmers was telling us through our interpreter that his horse had just died and he wouldn't be able to plow his fields without a new one, which he'd never be able to afford. So, what did you do, Jay?"

"Well, I gave the guy four hundred bucks when I thought no one was looking. I didn't really know how to tell him the money was for a new horse, so I tried to act it out."

"I looked over, and there's Jay doing the Gangnam Style dance for this farmer." Craig mimicked the dance in his seat, a comical feat for a man his age.

"I was trying to look like I was riding a horse!"

"He probably only took the money to get you to stop!"

"Worst thing, we came back a year later, and I

asked him about his horse. He had no idea what I was talking about. I hope my money went to a good cause."

The reminiscing continued over beers back at the hotel in Managua and extended late into the night. Unlike Craig and me, who were staying another full week in Nicaragua, Jay would be leaving in the morning back to blustery, cold South Dakota and his job as an accountant.

We said our goodbyes at six in the morning. I was sad to see him go. He had brought a consistency to the trip, as opposed to Craig's loose cannon personality. His sly wit, the kind that snuck up on you and was gone before you caught it if you weren't paying attention, would be missed.

As we waved goodbye to Jay, Sergio lifting his suitcase into the back of the pickup, I couldn't help but think again about the incredible amount of work our local friend put in to help the non-profit succeed. After our late night, he was back waiting outside the hotel before six in the morning. We'd been going dawn to dusk (or later) for a week straight, and I couldn't imagine he'd had any time to spend with his family since we'd arrived.

I was looking forward to getting an extra hour or two of sleep before we headed to the warehouse to pack for the day, but Craig had other ideas.

"Let's talk for a few minutes then I'll let you get back to bed," he said after Jay and Sergio pulled away. Knowing Craig, I had no doubt I wouldn't be getting back to sleep.

An hour and a half later, we were still talking, the cups of coffee in front of us having turned into a whole pot. We planned the rest of our trip, Craig's map spread across out table, bits of spilled breakfast scattered across the country.

We would start by visiting the communities of Masaya, Masatepe, and Jinotepe on the northern shores of Lake Nicaragua. On Saturday, we'd attend the Health Department's softball game hoping to sneak in another good word for our hospital project and replace my children's bats with the heaviest ones we had in the warehouse. The rest of Saturday would be spent in the warehouse, which had become such a mess of baseball equipment that finding matching anything was nearly impossible. The plan was to re-organize and take inventory of our remaining gear, divvying it up to be sure we would have enough for our final week of deliveries. Sunday would be spent on Omatepe, the small volcanic island in the middle of Lake Nicaragua where a small community of residents had squeezed themselves in between the two towering volcanoes. Monday would be more deliveries and meetings with our hospital project manager in the country, government contacts who had helped the container of baseball gear gain entry into the country tax-free, and a follow-up with the bishop. Tuesday, Wednesday, and Thursday would be spent in the farming communities with Scott Ramsdell, a South Dakotan agronomist who had been providing seeds, fertilizer, and education to local farmers for years with Craig. On Friday, I'd be on a plane back to whatever life awaited me in the United States.

Sergio returned from the airport and drove us to the warehouse. We spent the morning packing bags for ten teams, filling our truck, Orvin's SUV, and Jonathan's truck full to the last inch. When we finished, it took two people pushing together to get the back door of our truck to close on all the gear shoved inside. I realized we had a problem.

"Umm, Craig...where am I going to sit?" A literal wall of equipment filled my seat in the back of the truck.

We found room for me in Jonathan's truck under a pile of batting helmets. Our drive east out of Managua was relatively quiet. We gave up on small talk after a few minutes, my lack of Spanish proficiency making conversation a challenge for both of us. Instead, we listened to the radio, the Latino dance music much too loud and upbeat for the early morning. I tried to sleep uncomfortably against the window, my body contorted awkwardly to fit next to the batting helmets. The electronic beats and constant shouting from Pitbull made sleep nearly impossible.

Any hope I had left of dozing off disappeared completely when the excitable radio host proclaimed "y ahora, una cancion en Ingles!" and the familiar shrill intro of Justin Bieber's song Sorry filled the car.

It had been days since I had thought of her, the longest I had gone in over a year without having her on my mind, but Bieber's voice reset my count to zero immediately.

Like most girls in the United States, she loved Bieber like I loved her: hopelessly and unconditionally. I had heard his new CD on repeat for weeks prior to our breakup. Every time I saw her, she had it playing. Even with the chorus dubbed over in Spanish, I still knew the words.

"Is it too late to say sorry?" God, I hoped not.

I had saved paycheck after paycheck so I could buy

her a pair of tickets to his show in Minnesota, selling off personal belongings when my paychecks fell short. The final bill made the only two tickets I could find, in the very back of the nosebleeds as far away from the stage as physically possible, the single most expensive purchase I had made in my life.

Adding insult to injury, the tickets finally arrived in the mail two weeks after we had broken up. I thought briefly about re-selling them, but knowing they would make her smile, even if I wouldn't be there to see it, made the purchase worth it. I wrapped them in bright wrapping paper along with a copy of his new album and a calendar I had made weeks prior out of pictures of us for the upcoming new year. The title on the front, *All the days I will love you this year,* scrawled over a picture of us wrapped up in each other smiling broadly hurt to read but hadn't lost any of its truthfulness.

I had planned to just drop her gift off on her doorstep and not even ring the doorbell. The girl wanted space, and I was going to try to give it to her, no matter how pathetically bad I was at it. We had been connected from the minute we woke up until we fell asleep every day for a year and a half. Going cold turkey suddenly and not having any idea why was often more than I could take.

When I pulled up to her house, a dreary sleet was falling from the sky, guaranteeing we would not have a white Christmas the following day. Knowing the snowy rain would ruin my gift if I left it outside on the doorstep, I knocked, praying anyone but her would answer.

She appeared at the door a few moments later and stood staring at me through the blurry glass panel for what felt like the rest of my life before she opened the door.

"What are you doing here?" she demanded. I tried to explain that I was only there to deliver her gift, that I hadn't meant to knock but the rain, the rain, and boy, was it cold out, and wouldn't it be warmer next to her? I doubt I got a coherent sentence out.

"Well, come in then." I tried to tell her I just wanted to drop off the gifts and leave. She insisted. I tried to, but my resolve crumbled quicker than I could stutter anything else at her. I stepped inside.

She latched on to me in a hug that I never wanted to end. It wouldn't have had I been given a choice. She told me she missed me, she wanted to talk to me, she was glad to see me, she loved me. My voice was an echo of hers.

Of course, the silence resumed the following day and dragged on for nearly a month before she came wanting to get coffee the day I left for Nicaragua. In that time, she faded from a full-blown heart attack every time something made me think of her, which nearly everything caused, to a constant ache, a soreness in my chest.

It amazed me how many things on a daily basis reminded me of her. I hadn't realized how thoroughly connected our lives had been. The radio wasn't safe. Every song about love or heartbreak brought her to my mind. It got so bad that songs that didn't remind me of her reminded me of her, simply because they didn't remind me of her. I'm still trying to make sense of it. Ordinary things, like passing a windmill on the side of the road, me thinking of how terrified she had been of them, how she'd bury her head in my lap and refuse to come out until I promised it was gone, brought her to mind. Everything, everywhere, no matter how small, seemed to have some sort of connection to her for me.

Thankfully, Nicaragua was free of triggers for me, and I'd made it the last few days heartbreak free. I tried to wrestle my composure back from the radio as Sorry faded and Spanish pop music resumed with little luck.

My reprieve came when we pulled into Masaya and the hustle and bustle of the city distracted me out the window. Like any other Nicaraguan city, no discernible traffic rules existed in Masaya. Motorcycles swerved between cars, sometimes using the sidewalk if it looked faster. At every stoplight, flocks of people wandered between the cars peddling bags of nuts, snacks, newspapers, lottery tickets, and chewing gum. Men with massive bags of juice balanced on their heads knocked on our windows trying to get our attention to sell us a glass. Horse drawn carts held up traffic. Teenagers pedaled bicycle taxis, pedal bikes with a cart for passengers pulled behind, over cobblestone streets. There was something vintage about the whole scene.

In the center of the city, the houses were barred and barb-wired to deter thieves. As we headed towards the outskirts of town, the houses turned to sheet metal. There were no security precautions taken on these shanty houses. There was nothing worth stealing inside.

Our first stop was a dusty mess of a field. With no trees around to stop the wind, gusts coming off of the nearby Lake Nicaragua caused clouds of dirt to swirl in the air. Two teams of young ballplayers waited for us on the field, shielding their eyes to keep the dirt out. The youngsters were separated by age: the ten and under team in blue shirts and the thirteen and under team in white.

The Masaya Volcano, more a crater than a mountain, loomed over the field from a distance. When the wind got particularly strong, it would disappear behind a dusty haze. We lined up the two teams in single file lines, having gotten more efficient with our process after the first week. Craig handed the younger team new baseball pants, instructing each player to double back to the end of the line to receive the next piece of equipment. Maroon 'Golden Eagles' jerseys were next, followed by hats, gloves, and spikes. We repeated the process for the second team, the kids happily carrying their new gear to their coach's house in canvas dog food bags.

A young boy receives new baseball pants from Craig

We found our next team at the end of a long one-lane dirt road lined with jungle plants and spiked ferns. Far out of Masaya near the community of Masatepe, the little ball field was in the shadow of the volcano, close enough to the volcanic lagoon that we could hear the water lapping against the shores nearby.

It was probably the presence of the lagoon that allowed vegetation to grow dense on and around the baseball diamond. In Masaya, the field had been completely dirt. Here in Masatepe, lush shin-length green grass extended from home plate to the farthest reaches of the outfield.

There were only seven players waiting for us, leaned against a rusty chain-link backstop that had more holes in it than it did fence. The grass on the field was so long that my shoes disappeared beneath it when I walked across the infield to meet them. Six of the seven men were in jeans. One wore cargo shorts. They ranged from as young as seventeen into their forties.

"We're sorry our whole team could not be here today. We were the only ones who could get out of work to meet you," the eldest of them told us. We left them with two dozen brand new baseballs, two sets of catcher's gear, a glove for each player, a pile of cleats, and bright uniforms with 'Big Reds' on the front.

One of the older players, at least halfway through his thirties, gleefully tried on the catcher's masks we left.

"Finally! I have a mask!" he proclaimed. I couldn't help but wonder if it was a foul ball that had left his nose permanently crooked.

We shook hands with each player after posing for pictures with the equipment.

"Thanks to God that you are here. We do not have the resources here to play," the eldest told us as we prepared to leave. The catcher had put on a full set of catcher's gear and was having a teammate toss baseballs against his chest protector, laughing and saying, "It doesn't hurt now!"

In the grand scheme, we had done little to change the world, but for those seven men (the catcher's face especially), we had made a world of difference.

Our next stop was so far off the beaten path that it made the one-lane dirt road we had taken to get to the grass ball field feel like it had been Main Street in the middle of a bustling city. We drove so far into the country, bouncing on a crude, pothole-covered dirt path, that our radio lost reception completely. It was only after we passed a garbage dump, set so far into the country that citizens in nearby cities and communities wouldn't have to worry about seeing or smelling any of the waste, that we reached our destination.

And, my God, did the garbage smell. Most of it was smoldering when we passed, being burned to save space. Even with our windows rolled firmly up, the smell of putrid burning waste filled the truck, leaving me gagging in my seat.

A few miles past the dump, we pulled off the path onto a long dirt driveway. A square two-story school building waited at the end. A broken down swing set sat outside the school, flakes of rust peeling off of it in the wind. You could practically feel the tetanus in the air. Plastic bags blown from the garbage dump hung from the trees on the property. Pieces of trash, some still smoking, were scattered across the lawn. The smell of burning garbage carried on the wind was so strong that you could taste it on your tongue.

"How did you find this place?" I asked Sergio, one hand covering my mouth and nose to fight off the smell.

"They mailed me a cassette tape that they recorded directions on from Masatepe to here." Nicaraguan GPS, I suppose.

A cluster of teachers waited to welcome us to their school. We were given a tour of the facility, the classrooms rudimentary with nothing more than small wooden desks facing a single chalkboard.

The school doubled as an orphanage and offered meals for free to over three hundred children each day from nearby communities.

"Some of the children walk many miles to eat here each day. This far away from the city, there is a lot of poverty. Many kids wouldn't be able to eat or learn if not for this school," the director told us, our group, all of the baseball equipment we had brought, and all of the teachers squeezed into a small upstairs office.

"Thank you for this equipment," the physical education teacher told us. He was only slightly older than me, in slacks and a black button-up. "In the past, I have always had to improvise in my gym classes. The kids love to play baseball, but we have nothing to play with. If you noticed outside, the trees have no low branches left on them. We have removed them all to use as baseball bats. This school year, the students will be able to play for real." There was a genuine happiness in his voice and spread across his face.

"Can you do me one favor?" Craig asked. "Please make sure the girls also have access to the equipment."

"That won't be a problem, I promise. There is quite

a rivalry here when we play baseball between the girls and the boys. The girls play harder and often win."

Craig was clearly pleased by the answer and knowing that both boys and girls would be given the opportunity to play in the future. We left the school and drove until the smell of burning garbage faded before stopping for lunch at the kind of local restaurant where you washed your hands in a bucket after using the bathroom. While we ate, Orvin regaled us with stories from his real estate business.

Of course, to call Orvin a real estate agent would be like calling Sergio our chauffeur. Both were so much more than their titles suggested. Orvin sold extravagant beachside estates on Nicaragua's western coast to rich retired foreigners, serving as their tour guide, translator, and transportation while they were in the country. Legend has it that he is so well-connected within the country that a wealthy customer once demanded to speak with the president of Nicaragua to discuss construction laws and Orvin had the meeting set up within the week. For the non-profit, he had provided numerous baseball contacts, including setting up initial meetings with Nemesio and Dennis Martinez during Craig's first visits to the country to deliver equipment.

"You know, Craig, you could be like the rest of my American clients, coming here to retire in a big house by the ocean." Orvin was wearing his typical outfit: a flashy polo shirt and aviator sunglasses. "But instead you come here to help our country. I had to leave my house at five this morning to get to Managua in time to meet you at the warehouse, but it's more than worth it to me to be a part of all the good you do for Nicaragua."

Craig paused before responding. "I asked myself

'what should I do with my life now?' a few years back. I could be sitting on a beach, and I don't blame people who choose to do that, they earned it. But, I would rather come to Nicaragua and do what I think is important."

The afternoon following our local lunch was easily one of the highlights of a trip filled with them for me. We drove west to Jinotepe, a colorful colonial-era town squarely in the middle of the strip of land separating Lake Nicaragua from the Pacific Ocean, just miles from either body of water.

A small baseball academy waited for us, two games going on simultaneously on the academy's one field. One game was being played on the actual diamond, a field with bases and a pitcher's mound flanked by a grandstand. The other game was being played in the right field corner, the outfielders from the two separate games standing next to each other facing opposite directions.

We were greeted by a young, muscular coach in a Nike shirt and orange Houston Astros hat. Just looking at him, it was clear he had been a ballplayer and a good one at that. He introduced himself as Marwin, and we stood in deep left field under the shade provided by a small school building that also doubled as the outfield fence and watched the two games. I asked Marwin who he had played for, hoping to be in the presence of another former major leaguer. Both his build and the way he carried himself made me sure he had once been a star.

"I always dreamed of playing baseball. My whole life I wanted to play. I just never had the opportunity. That's why I'm here working with these kids, to make sure they get that chance."

While we talked, frantic shouting in Spanish came from the main field and we looked up just in time to watch a ball sail over us and land on the roof of the school building directly behind us.

"Home run!" Marwin proclaimed as the left fielder jumped to grab on to the overhanging roof and pull himself up to retrieve the ball. A bulky teenager was rounding second base in a slow home run trot. "He's one of our best players. Plays first base and can hit the ball a mile. I'm hoping to get a scout out here to watch him play."

Marwin figured the home run made for a good stopping point and called for the teams to suspend their games and join us in the outfield. A mass of fifty-plus ballplayers formed in front of us. Marwin introduced us to his teams, and Craig spoke to them briefly before turning to me.

"Dan, why don't you talk to them this time?"

Before I could protest, Marwin introduced me to the crowd.

"This is Daniel Venn. He is a college pitcher in the United States. Does anyone know what comes after college baseball?"

"Las Ligas Grandes!" *The Major Leagues!*

The kids were wide-eyed when I stepped into the middle of the crowd to speak, still nervously deciding what to say. I almost laughed at the exaggerated introduction I had received. If only they had any idea just how mediocre my baseball career had been. By my senior year, I was a mop-up reliever at the lowest level of college ball, spending more time in the trainer's room with two tears in my shoulder than on the mound. I couldn't count my college ERA on one hand.

But the kids didn't know that, so why let them down?

"Hello, my name is Daniel Venn. I'm a pitcher in the United States. I'm very happy to be back here in Nicaragua. Years ago, I had the opportunity to pitch here, and it is wonderful to be back."

"With what team?" a kid shouted out in Spanish.

"I played in Rivas." Excitement ran through the crowd, and a few kids whispered "Los Gigantes!" to the teammates around them, thinking I had played for the city's professional team, the reigning Nicaraguan League champion. I continued in my broken, choppy sentences in Spanish, urging the kids to keep working hard, ending by saying that I hoped to play against them in the United States one day.

Craig addressing the players at the academy

I received a loud round of applause when I finished, a reception I was almost ashamed to get with the amount of exaggeration I had told them. Craig took back over after me, giving his usual spiel on the non-profit and the donated equipment. He began distributing the gear to each of the four teams. Photographs and niceties followed.

I knew the process was important. The speeches, the handshakes, the pictures were all part of being respectful and following local customs. The photographs on our cameras would go to our donors in the States, showing them the impact their donations had made and hopefully leading them to give again in the future. But, after a week straight of ceremonies and pleasantries, of being so close to baseball but never actually getting to play, I had had enough.

I abandoned my post sorting out gloves for each team and got my backpack out of Jonathan's truck. Every morning of the trip, I had slipped my own baseball glove and ball inside, hoping to get the chance to use them.

"Who wants to play catch with me?" I asked the players from the youngest of the four teams. They had been first in line to receive gear and were crowded around their haul excitedly trying on gloves, hats, and jerseys. Multiple hands shot up immediately, and there was a mad scramble to grab a glove from the donated pile and join me.

"Wait, wait!" Marwin scolded the kids light-heartedly. He had been trying to sort and distribute each piece of gear to the players based on size. He pointed to one young player, no more than twelve years in age. "This is our best pitching prospect. He will play catch with you."

The kid's eyes lit up as Marwin handed him a brand new glove and walked him over to me. We shook hands and began tossing the ball lightly back and forth. I hadn't thrown a ball in months, and even when I had, I hadn't meant to. The previous summer, I had been sitting in the stands after watching a game played by my hometown's amateur team, chatting with a former teammate who was still playing, and was spotted by the coach.

"Venn, you're in town?" he asked. "Got plans Friday night?" I told him I was planning to be back to watch their game against our crosstown rival, baseball games being about the only form of entertainment in our nothing farm town. "Be here. You're pitching."

I had sworn off playing baseball after walking off the field following the fifth inning of my last college game over a year prior. My senior season had been a disaster. We set a new school record for most losses in a season. I barely saw the field, my wrecked shoulder keeping me off the mound most days, my performance forcing me off quickly during my rare appearances. As the only graduating senior pitcher, I was given a pity start the last game of the season. It was a meaningless, non-conference game, but to me, knowing it was probably the last time I'd ever see the field, it was Game 7.

Somehow, I guiled my way through five innings, effectively doubling my innings total for the entire season, on what was left of my fastball and an even slower change-up. A diving stop by our third baseman saved me in a bases loaded jam to end the fifth. I had run out of steam innings ago, everything I threw getting hit hard, but somehow the ball kept finding our fielders' gloves. I knew walking off the field, watching my teammates swarm our third baseman with high-fives, that I was officially done.

"You got one more in you?" our pitching coach asked when I reached the dugout.

"I'm done, Coach." He didn't catch the finality of my statement.

"You sure you don't want to try and finish this thing off?"

"No, I'm done." I looked down at my right shoulder, my arm hanging limp, the pain that had crawled under my shoulder blade and hung around for years on fire again. "With baseball."

And I was for over a year. The only time I picked up a ball following my last college game and before appearing with my hometown's amateur team on a whim was to lightly toss batting practice pitches to the team of seventh graders I was pressed into coaching while student teaching. Even that was quickly stopped after one cocky little adolescent begged me to throw him one pitch as hard as I could with Gatorade for the whole team on the line if he hit it. I accidentally put a fastball in the middle of his back. It took three teammates to carry him off the field. They got their Gatorade, mainly because I wanted to avoid any potential lawsuits.

I had tried so hard to go beyond baseball, to grow up and leave the game behind. Besides my short relapse with the amateur team, never more than an inning or two at a time, I had effectively cut the game out of my life.

There was no better place to get the game back,

tossing a ball back and forth with a twelve-year-old on a field in Central America. More kids joined in on our game after a few minutes, and I soon had a line of ballplayers taking turns to catch a throw from me and hurl it back. Our Nicaraguan staff—Sergio, Orvin, and Jonathan—grabbed gloves and joined us when they finished handing out equipment. Even Marwin joined in, imploring me to throw one to him hard and getting into a catcher's crouch. I did my best.

"Come on, really throw one hard to me!" he called out after I went through my full windup and gave him all I had.

"That was hard," I responded meekly. I could tell he was disappointed. Even he had believed I was a real baseball player. But, it did little to deter our fun. He brought his pitchers to me, and I did my best to help each one of them with their mechanics, trying my best to translate all the clichés I had heard from pitching coaches over the years into Spanish.

An impromptu infield-outfield practice broke out, Sergio hitting grounders and towering flies to the kids. Marwin and I roved the field, jumping in front of kids to field ground balls and using our height to steal fly balls from them. Marwin was ecstatic, finally getting his chance to play, as was I, finally getting to play again.

The adults were still out there, playing like we were kids, long after the players' parents came to pick them up. A few of the kids came back on their bikes after their parents brought them home. We stayed playing catch until Craig called out that we had to leave to get back to Managua before it got too dark out. The sun was already starting to fade behind the horizon.

119

I high-fived the kids I had been playing with and headed for the truck, giddy from getting to be on the field again for a few hours.

"Señor, su pelota!" one of the kids shouted to me, holding my ball up to show me I had forgotten it. He tossed the ball to me.

"Keep it!" I shouted in English and threw it back to him. As we drove away, the kids were still standing in the outfield playing catch as the sun set behind them.

Chapter 9

I stood balancing precariously on the toilet, one foot on each side of the bowl, doing my best not to fall in. Wouldn't that be a story to tell? Falling in, getting myself stuck, and having to be extracted from my hotel room's toilet in the middle of the night would rank near the top of embarrassing things I've done abroad. Of course, it would never top using my pants as a toilet in public in Costa Rica, not that it was an experience I ever wanted to best.

There was probably a more efficient way for me to wash my clothes than standing straddling the toilet seat, but it was conveniently squeezed between the tiny bathroom's sink and shower. I had the sink plugged with a pair of socks and filled with soapy water. From my perch on the toilet, I could wash my clothes in the sink to my right and rinse them in the shower to my left without getting too wet myself. The floor was covered ankle-deep with sudsy water, and I had slipped repeatedly walking from the sink to the shower, making the toilet seem like the safest option.

Of course, given how dirty and sweaty I was following our long Saturday, I probably should have just worn my clothes into the shower and washed myself along with them. We had begun the day at the Health Department's softball game, sitting in foul territory with the team, small-talking sports and public health. They took the field in the new uniforms we had brought them and were thrilled to see the new, heavier bats.

A MINSA batter awaits a pitch

They had told us that their league was overly-competitive during our initial meeting, and their six-foot-tall trophy should have been enough to convince me. Any doubt I had about how serious they took their softball disappeared when I had to present the bats to the umpire before the game to be weighed and inspected to make sure they hadn't been tampered with or corked. Each player was required to show both their government ID badge and driver's license, a league official holding the cards up to check the pictures against each player's face prior to the game to be sure no team tried to bring in a ringer to help them win.

They played fast, intense softball, nothing like the beer league games I had watched in the United States. Pitchers, catchers, and batters argued balls and strikes with the umpire. Players slid hard into second base, upending infielders to break up potential double plays. Coaches took mound visits to talk strategy with their pitchers. It was entertaining to watch, but part of me felt like we were wasting time we could have been spending bringing more children more equipment. Craig seemed to read my mind.

"I wish we were out in the communities right now. But, if being here helps us get a hospital into the country, it will have a far greater impact on the people of Nicaragua than our baseball equipment ever could."

Despite a decade-long government initiative to improve health care outcomes in the country, Nicaragua still has a frighteningly poor health care system according to studies conducted by the World Bank. The infant mortality rate in Nicaragua is still three to four times as great as the rate in the United States. Many of those deaths are from causes that would be preventable with improved medical technology and improved access to health care. One in three children in Nicaragua suffer from anemia, an iron-deficiency caused by poor diet that impairs cognitive, motor, and language development as well as educational outcomes. The rate in the United States is in the low single digits.

Private clinics provide high quality health care in

Nicaragua, but only a small percentage of the country has access to health insurance. The vast majority of Nicaraguans are left paying medical expenditures out of pocket, making the private clinics only accessible to the rich. Public hospitals, where the majority of citizens receive their care, are often underfunded and understaffed and lack twenty-first century medical technology.

The only requirement Craig made to the Health Department in our initial visit was that his donated hospital equipment would go to public hospitals and not private clinics. Simply put, the children of Nicaragua would never be able to play baseball if they were not healthy. The hospital project would help make that a possibility for many.

Our presence at the game seemed to help re-affirm our relationship with the Health Department. Following the game, the players invited us to join them for food and drink along the first baseline with their families. They asked to take pictures with us, holding up new bats and gloves and pointing to their donated uniforms, arms draped over our shoulders. Conversation in Spanish drifted from the formal, professional 'usted' to the amicable 'tu'. We were again assured that we would receive their help if we needed it in the future as we headed back to the truck in the early afternoon.

The rest of the day was spent in the warehouse. From just after noon until well after eight in the evening, we hauled baseball equipment back and forth in the hot warehouse. We dug through and crawled over mountains of bats, balls, gloves, and uniforms, organizing each into separate piles. We packed bags for each of our remaining visits. A separate pile was started with softballs, batting gloves, spikes and tennis shoes, batting tees, and other equipment we thought would be useful to the softball academy we had visited. Johnny Alvarez drove up from Rivas, working alongside us well into the evening in exchange for leaving with his car packed full of gear for his fledgling academy. Sergio, Luis, and a handful of youth from the local Lutheran church sweated next to us for hours, the kids receiving nothing more than a hat from the pile in return for their help at the end of the day.

Craig and I had eaten breakfast before seven in the morning at the hotel. Beyond the snacks we were offered at the softball game, we didn't eat again until well after eight that night. I thought about complaining as the day went on, hunger gnawing inside my stomach, but felt guilty for even having the thought as I watched our local helpers work through dinner time and into the night without as much as a break for water.

When we finally did leave, the warehouse as cleaned up as it could be given the incredible amount of gear that still remained, bags packed for a 4:30 AM wake up call to catch the morning ferry to Omatepe Island, we were too exhausted and sweaty to consider sitting down for dinner at a restaurant. Instead, we raided the nearest gas station for food and drinks. My dinner consisted of a nutritious mix of plantain chips, candy-coated peanuts, chocolate chip cookies, Fresco Leche chocolate milk, and as many bottles of water as I could carry. I was dizzy from the heat we had worked in all day, and it took three full bottles of water just to feel right again.

Despite how tired I was, I struggled to fall asleep after sharing a romantic dinner with the plump woman in the painting above the bed in my hotel room. It wasn't my thoughts that kept me up, like they had for a month straight, but the smell coming from my dirty clothes pile in the far corner of my room. I had only brought a small carry-on suitcase for the trip, fitting a few days' worth of t-shirts and shorts inside, and had been wearing the same outfits on repeat since we had arrived.

So, I found myself standing on the toilet in the bathroom, washing my clothes in the sink and rinsing them in the shower. I couldn't help but make eye contact with my reflection in the small mirror hanging above the sink as I worked. I had been avoiding my reflection for weeks as I got sadder and sadder following the breakup, afraid of what I would see. I couldn't avoid myself in the little bathroom. There was a hardness in my face that hadn't been there before. Something was missing in my eyes.

Although the shower water wasn't heated, it sat in a tank on the hotel's roof all day and was at least lukewarm after spending the day in the sun. It was enough, combined with my breath in the crowded space, to cloud the mirror. When my face faded behind the fog on the mirror, I used a finger to draw a smiley face in the place mine had been. Laughing to myself, I drew a little mustache above my lopsided smile. For years, I had waited for puberty to kick in and allow me to grow something that resembled facial hair. Peach fuzz would have been enough to make me celebrate.

Although I could have done No-Shave November year-round without anyone noticing, I still shaved often anyways simply to make myself feel like a man. I had elected to leave my razor at home during the Nicaragua trip just to see what would happen. As I stared into the mirror, I was surprised to see that a dark, patchy mustache had appeared on my upper lip. I tried to wash it off, figuring it was just dirt, but it didn't budge. As proud of myself as I was, I made a mental note to find a razor as soon as possible. I didn't know if there was an international version of To Catch A Predator in Nicaragua, but I was sure looking at my reflection that if I let the mustache grow any more and kept trying to work with children, I would find out.

Even standing on the toilet, trying to stay dry with water splashing from the sink and the shower and dripping off the clothes I held was impossible. I took my bar of soap and ran it from the shoulders of my shirt to the bottom of my shorts and then took them off and tossed them into the shower. Even my boxers were soaked, so I took them off and tossed them in as well. Weeks ago, I was wearing neatly-pressed dress shirts and ties, going to a nine-to-five job, reading a newspaper over breakfast in the morning, and coming home to a kiss from the future missus at night. Now, I was standing naked on a toilet seat in Nicaragua, washing my clothes in the shower, unemployed and single with no plan beyond tomorrow. How had I fallen this far?

Had I really fallen at all?

Chapter 10

We filed sleepily to the truck a few minutes after four in the morning. Sergio was waiting outside the hotel already with Luis, whose taxi we had filled with gear the night before to maximize how much equipment we could take to Omatepe with us. Craig had never visited the small island before and wanted to make up for leaving them out in the past with a large donation.

The ferry to the island ran on an erratic schedule, leaving at the captain's convenience sometime in the morning and returning to the mainland late in the day. We would be getting there as early as we could to ensure we would be able to get tickets and, if possible, get our truck on board. According to Sergio, the ferry to the island carried a few vehicles to and from the island each day on a first-come, first-served basis. Being able to bring our truck to the island, drive it to our stops, and return to the mainland with it would be ridiculously more convenient than having to carry all of our equipment by hand to and across the island.

We arrived at the lakeside city of Granada at seven in the morning and found it nearly deserted. Lake Nicaragua, over one hundred miles in length, stretched as far as I could see in either direction. The freshwater lake is not only the largest in Central America but the home of a diverse collection of aquatic species. Most believe the lake was at one time part of the ocean before being cut off by a volcanic eruption from one of the two volcanoes that make up Omatepe. Once separated, sharks, tarpon, and swordfish from the ocean were trapped inside the lake, adapting over time to the fresh water, making the lake the only freshwater body of water containing oceanic animal life.

We searched up and down the boardwalk bordering the lake for the ticket office only to find it closed. Rows of small restaurants and stores lined both sides of the narrow street, all closed as well. We decided to make a quick return stop at the Belen daycare outside of town. While organizing the warehouse, a bag of toddler-sized baseball bats and gloves had turned up, the perfect gift for the kids at the daycare to go with their new books.

Our stop there was quick. Sergio had warned us that the owners of the daycare might not yet be up, it being only seven AM and the weekend, but both were standing outside when we pulled up.

"Good morning!" they called when they saw us climb out of the truck. "We're butchering an armadillo! Would you like some?"

We unanimously elected to drop off the baseball equipment and get out of there as quickly as possible before we found ourselves with plates of armadillo meat in our hands and no polite way to escape. I had eaten guinea pig, live ants, cow testicle, and dried blood (the last two at the same time!) on previous travels and normally thoroughly enjoy trying new foods, but there was nothing appetizing about starting the day off with a culinary adventure before even having breakfast.

When we returned to the shores of Lake Nicaragua, we found the port starting to wake up. The ticket office was open but not selling tickets. A strong wind had picked up on the lake and white-capped waves were making it too dangerous for the ferry to cross safely. We were instructed to keep checking back to see if the ferry would be canceled for the day.

We wandered the beach, taking photos of the two volcanoes on Omatepe and watching the waves crash into the shore, before settling in at a small beach-side bar to wait out the winds. Shortly after nine, the first round of beers arrived at the table.

"You know, this is a blessing in disguise," Craig said, sipping from a green Toña beer bottle. "We've been working so hard and going so fast, having a little time to slow down might be just what we need."

Our conversation drifted aimlessly from one subject to another with Sergio and Luis. We talked about politics, both Nicaraguan and American. We had to switch from beer to rum to get through a discussion on the legitimacy of Donald Trump's candidacy in the upcoming presidential election. Sergio and Luis told us more about their lives. Sergio was studying to become a pastor. Luis was trying to support his wife on his taxi driver's salary.

When Sergio and Luis went to check back with the ticket office, Craig and I talked baseball and travels. His son had been a spectacular pitcher, both in college and in professional independent baseball. We talked attitudes for pitchers on the mound, performance enhancing drugs (both of us against them, obviously), Pete Rose's Hall of Fame candidacy (both of us for it), and how easy it is to travel the world if you try.

Craig told me stories from his adventures around the world. When he was my age, he made a living smuggling and selling products in street markets around the world, bouncing from country to country, selling cigars and watches and trinkets he bought in one country in the next he visited. From the first time I had spoken to him on the phone prior to the trip, I had sensed he had the ability to sell anything to anyone (like convincing me to drive across the country and hop on a plane to Nicaragua with two men I had never met on two days' notice), a skill he had developed in black markets and on streets all around the world.

He told stories from cities and countries I hadn't even heard of. The man's life could easily be a book of its own, each chapter a different adventure in a different region of the world, and he would probably run out of paper before he ran out of stories.

Sergio and Luis returned having had no luck. The ferry's launch kept getting pushed back. One person told them it would go at eleven that morning. Another said one in the afternoon. A third thought it wouldn't leave at all. With little choice but to keep talking and drinking until we found out more, we did both wholeheartedly.

Craig and I had discussed steroids in baseball while our two friends had been looking for tickets. Of course, we were both very much against them. For me, they had taken down nearly every player I had looked up to growing up and had left me skeptical of any player who put up good numbers since. But, I was curious to know what Nicaraguan fans thought of them. A few years back, Everth Cabrera, then a Padres shortstop and the pride of Nicaraguan baseball, the only player from the country to ever be selected for the All Star Game besides Dennis Martinez, had been suspended 50 games for steroid use.

"Of course we're against them," Sergio told me. "They're cheating, and they're wrong. But, I think we can understand here why a player would use them. It's so hard to make it in baseball coming from Nicaragua. If that's what it takes to make it to the United States or to make it to the major leagues, I can see how it would be a tough decision. We were disappointed when we found out about Everth, but it made sense too."

I slipped the same question in at the end of my interview with international scout Nick Holmes. He was more frank with his explanation.

"Kids from the United States have options if they don't make it in baseball. If they get cut, they can still go to school and get a job and do just fine for themselves. An international player from a poor country doesn't have that option. If they get cut, they're on the next plane back home, and most of them don't have the education or skills to be successful once they get there. It's baseball or nothing. If you tell a kid he just needs to stick a needle in his ass and he'll keep getting a paycheck and be able to support his family, well, you can see the temptation."

Statistically, that temptation seems to exist. Over sixty percent of the players suspended by Major League Baseball under their performance enhancing drugs policy have been players born in Latin American countries. Beyond the sheer difficulty of reaching the majors from these countries, many factors may contribute to these numbers: lack of regulation of substances banned in the United States in foreign countries, over-the-counter availability of anabolic steroids in many Latin American pharmacies, inferior education, and pressure from buscones and trainers.

I delicately asked Marvin Benard about the number of Latin American players suspended, and he was quick to caution me about assigning the problem to one population of ballplayers.

"The stats may be deceiving. I don't think Latin players are *using* these substances at a higher rate than any other demographic. I think they are just getting *caught* at a higher rate for various reasons. The sheer pressure of playing and wanting to succeed at the highest level in baseball makes PED use tempting to all players."

Almost ironically, following our conversation on PEDs, Sergio and Luis found tickets for the ferry that turned out to be just as fake as the sluggers I had grown up watching. We had moved to a small restaurant down the boardwalk to have lunch, and a man came in selling tickets to the ferry he claimed would be leaving at two in the afternoon. We bought one for each of us and a pass to bring our truck on board, raising our glasses at the table in celebration of finally knowing there would be a ferry leaving and we would be on it.

The scalper was right about the ferry leaving at two. Unfortunately, we weren't on it. The security guard checking tickets at the end of the long dock extending to where the ferry waited took one look at our tickets and declared them fakes. We had been had and watched scornfully as the boat headed to the island without us.

Thankfully, the guard felt sorry for us and helped arranged for us to get spot on a different ferry leaving later that afternoon. It would take us to the wrong port on a completely different side of the island than we needed to be on, but it would take us to the island.

We made it to the island in the late afternoon. As frustrated as we were, it was impossible not to notice how beautiful the place was. Green palm trees dotted long sand beaches. The twin volcanoes towered over everything, incredible up close. There were almost no cars on the narrow roads. Most people walked or rode pedal bicycles. A few motorcycles shared the streets with the pedestrians.

One of Omatepe's two volcanoes from the port

The island reminded me a lot of Samoa, the beautiful tropical paradise I had been sent to by the Peace Corps before I had up and quit for the girl.

Thankfully for the people of Omatepe, a tourist economy thrived on the island, helping them escape the crushing poverty that made Samoa a place that required assistance from the Peace Corps despite its natural beauty.

We were able to reach the coach of the teams we were scheduled to meet over a shaky cell phone signal. He gave us a location he would meet us at, halfway between where we had landed and where we were supposed to be. We found him sitting on the side of the road a half hour later.

"How far is it to your community?" I asked after we introduced ourselves. The coach, Efrain, was dark-skinned and well-mustached, approaching fifty years of age.

"About twelve kilometers from here." I looked around to see where he had parked his car, or his motorcycle, or at least his pedal bike, but found nothing.

"How did you get this far?" I asked.

"I walked." He said it like it should have been obvious. "I was going to walk all the way to the port to meet you, but I needed to take a break. I'm sorry I didn't make it." He had already walked over seven miles to meet us and had planned to double that just to get some baseball equipment.

We had left Luis' taxi on the mainland, the second ferry only having room for one vehicle. All the gear that we brought in Luis' taxi was now tied to the roof of the pickup, the bed completely full. With Luis, myself, and a pile of equipment in the back seat, there was little room for Efrain, and we hastily tried to rearrange so he could join us in the truck. He insisted he would walk back so we would not be inconvenienced or uncomfortable on the trip.

We eventually convinced him to accept a ride in the back of the pickup truck on top of all of the baseball equipment. He rode it like a king on a throne back to his community. All of it would be going to his players.

When we arrived, a herd of young ballplayers waited for us at the community's only field. We had expected to be on a ferry early in the morning and hadn't arrived until well after dark, yet every one of Efrain's players was waiting when we arrived. Their parents had given up and gone home hours ago, but the youngsters' faith had not wavered.

As Craig gave his customary introductory speech to the players, a high-pitched electrical shriek cut through the island air, and the streetlight we were standing under went dark. All of the lights in the community followed immediately after, and we were left in pitch darkness.

"Happens all the time," Efrain told us. "The electricity here isn't very reliable."

He sent his players home to get flashlights. They scampered off, each returning in minutes with a light. By the glow of their small flashlights alone, we unloaded the gear and presented it to the children. It didn't take much light to see their smiles.

As we handed out the gear, I chatted with Efrain. After over a week in the country, my Spanish had started coming back to me. I had even caught myself thinking in Spanish the night before while in bed. Even in my head, it was broken Spanish but so were most of my thoughts. It was enough to understand Efrain.

"I'm so glad you are here. For all of these

children." He gestured at the young ballplayers crowded around us. "We have just five bats, and we share gloves with the teams we play."

When we finished unloading and distributing, the kids carried all of the gear to Efrain's house to be stored until their next practice. We continued talking as we walked there, watching the kids happily shouldering heavy bags of bats and balls.

"I chose to become involved with baseball here because it helps the kids so much. It keeps them off drugs. It keeps them off the streets. It gives them a reason to go to school and stay out of trouble." It was a refrain I had heard on repeat at almost every community we had visited.

Craig handing out equipment in the dark

I helped the kids carry the bags into Efrain's house when we arrived. His home was humble, a few small brick rooms. His bedroom had just a hammock instead of a bed. As we finished stacking the gear inside, he offered to let us stay for the night. There would be no ferry going back to the mainland until the morning, and he would vacate his own home for the night and sleep on the floor at one of his player's house so we would have as much room as possible.

The offer was impossibly gracious and not one we were willing to accept, especially given how far Efrain had walked to meet us and how tired he must be at the end of the day. The least we could do was let the man sleep in his own hammock.

We found rooms at a local hotel. The electricity was still out and running water on the island had gone with it, but they had beds and lit a fire in the kitchen so they could make us dinner. We ate in the dark happily, enjoying good food in the company of good friends at the end of a good day.

"Who do you think is winning the game?" Craig asked me as we finished dinner and sat at the table talking about the day over a few more beers.

"What game?" I tried to think what he could be talking about.

"The Super Bowl is tonight, you know that right?"

I hadn't missed a Super Bowl broadcast in my life, yet in the midst of all our adventure and traveling in Nicaragua, I had completely forgotten it was taking place.

"Is this worth missing it for?" Craig asked, seeing the shock on my face when I realized the biggest game of the year was going on and I wasn't watching it.

I just laughed in response. It wasn't even a question.

Chapter 11

I was jolted awake by a blinding light. Rapid-fire Spanish filled our hotel room. Was Luis, my roommate for the night, talking in his sleep? A second voice responded. There was definitely more than one person in our room.

I covered my eyes, blinking rapidly to try to get them to adjust from pitch-dark to the bright light. A third voice had joined the first two. Were we being robbed? I wasn't awake enough to translate what the voices were saying, and my eyes were stubbornly taking their time adjusting. The voices were unfamiliar and unfriendly.

I had almost been robbed once in Costa Rica, a man following me down the sidewalk menacingly, gaining on me, when I was foolish enough to walk home after dark. I was an easy target. I was alone, it was late at night, and my bag slung over my shoulder would have made for an easy grab-and-go robbery. Thankfully, I had been on my way home from baseball practice and had a baseball bat in my bag. Pulling it out was enough to deter the thief. Luckily, he had never seen me hit before or he would have known I had no idea how to use the bat I spun and brandished at him.

I had to give it to these thieves, breaking into our hotel room in the middle of the night was an intelligent plan. Luis and I had carelessly left our phones and wallets on our bedside tables, and the thieves could be in and out with them in seconds. I'm not sure if I agreed with turning on the lights and talking loudly while pulling off the heist, but as someone with no experience in thievery, who was I to judge?

The ceiling finally came into focus as my eyes started to accept the light. Turning on the lights had taken the element of surprise away but also made it much easier to quickly locate valuable items sitting out. It had woken me up but also disoriented me, giving them more than enough time to get away. I swept the room quickly with my eyes. Empty. They were already gone.

"Luis!" I hissed somewhere between a whisper and a scream. He was still fast asleep in his bed, snoring slightly. My wallet and phone were sitting right where I had left them. The voices had faded out, but they came back strong. Had the robbers returned?

I turned towards the door to face them. No one was there. A trio of talking heads were arguing with each other on the television by the door. The screen flashed to highlights from the Super Bowl.

And then, it all made sense. The power had come back on, hence the lights. The TV must have been on when the lights went out, and it had come back on with the power. I felt stupid for panicking, but at least, after watching for a few minutes, the TV told me that the Broncos had won the Super Bowl. I flipped the lights and TV off and went back to sleep.

It felt like just minutes passed before Craig was knocking on our door urging us to get out of bed and to the port to catch the ferry to the mainland. I reached for my phone to check the time only to find it long dead. Judging by the light peeking in through the window, it was early morning.

We had planned to catch the morning ferry to the island, distribute the gear, return to the mainland on the afternoon ferry, and be back in Managua by nightfall. I hadn't packed anything more than my notebooks, camera, and baseball glove in my backpack. The shirt I had worn to the island was the only one I didn't wash in my hotel bathroom, leaving one out just in case my laundry didn't dry in time. I had worn it multiple days on the trip, and it was no longer suitable to wear in public in both appearance and smell.

The only other thing in my bag was a yellow youth-sized mesh baseball uniform with 'Mitchell Sluggers' scrawled on the front. The Sluggers, a team from South Dakota, had sent the jersey with Craig, promising they would make a large donation in the future if he returned with pictures of Nicaraguan ballplayers in their jersey. At each of our stops, we had outfitted a player in the jersey and snapped a photo. I probably had just as many pictures of future Mitchell Sluggers on my camera than I had of anything else.

"Well, looks like the Sluggers are getting their best endorsement today," I muttered to myself, pulling the child-sized jersey over my head. Although saying that I'm much more than child-sized myself would be an outright lie, the jersey ended at my belly button, leaving a pale swath of midriff exposed. The jersey was tight on my shoulders, constricting my arms and making me fear that any movement too sudden would rip the sleeves right off.

"That's a good look for you," Craig teased when I emerged from the room.

"I feel scandalous showing off so much skin." I had my hat pulled down as low as it would go over my eyes, trying to cover as much of my face as possible. There's nothing better than going out in public in a foreign country wearing a belly shirt.

"Come on, girls love a good tummy tan line!" Somehow, after ten days in the hot Central American sun, I hadn't tanned at all. I was still the same bright white the snow had been back in Minnesota. Craig, on the other hand, looked like he was made of leather, his face turning a dark brown after just a few days in the country.

We hurried across town in the truck with our fingers crossed that the ferry wouldn't be delayed again. We had a pair of meetings set up in Managua in the afternoon, one with the bishop and one with a high-ranking government official who had signed off on our container being tax-free. If we didn't make it back in time to attend, we'd have to choose between leaving Tuesday morning for the farming projects in northern Nicaragua or sticking around to get the meetings done.

We arrived at the port within minutes of the ferry's scheduled departure. Thankfully, it was on time, and tickets were still available. Unfortunately, there was no space left for our truck.

We stood huddled on the dock trying to devise a

plan. Craig needed to be present at the meetings. Hands needed to be shook. Bills needed to be paid. Without Sergio translating, Craig would be useless at the meetings. I couldn't drive the truck. I was horrified enough sitting in the backseat in the lawless Nicaragua traffic.

"Me," Luis said in English, pointing to himself. He spoke to Sergio in Spanish.

"Luis says he'll stay with the truck and bring it back to Managua as soon as he can get it on a ferry." Luis was holding out the keys to his taxi. "We'll drive his taxi to our meetings and to the farming projects if he's still stuck here tomorrow."

It was a big sacrifice from Luis. His taxi was his career. If we ended up having to drive his taxi to the farming projects, he'd miss a full week of work. The job wasn't a particularly lucrative one to start with, and with a family at home, risking missing a paycheck could not have been an easy decision. With the guard on the ferry shouting at us to either get on now or stay behind, we didn't have time to think of a better plan. We each shook hands with Luis. If we did end up taking his taxi to the farming projects, we'd be there through Thursday night and then would fly out early Friday morning and probably wouldn't see him again.

Once on board the ferry, we found every seat taken and people standing in the aisles of the cabin. We settled for a spot on the floor outside against the railing on the side of the boat, our feet dangling over the side. It may have been soggier and less comfortable than the seats in the passenger cabin, but the view could not be beat. For the entirety of the trip, I slowly watched the twin volcanoes get smaller and smaller behind us and enjoyed the spray from the warm waves on my face.

We raced back to Managua in Luis' taxi. Taxi drivers are notorious in Nicaragua for reckless, high-speed driving, and Sergio took full advantage of the opportunity. We arrived in Managua in record time, more nauseous from swerving through traffic than we had been after being and tossed and turned by the waves of Lake Nicaragua on the ferry.

"That was fun!" Sergio proclaimed as we climbed out of the truck inside the gates of the Ministry of Sport government complex. I was too busy trying to find solid ground to stand on to respond.

We probably should have known something was up when our government contact insisted that we didn't meet him in his office, directing us instead to a picnic table at a small roadside cafe far away from any of the government buildings. He brought with him a stack of paperwork, all of the documents and receipts he had accumulated while pushing our project through the bureaucracy.

He went over them one-by-one with Craig, explaining the process and pointing out how much each step had cost. His stack of papers had everything from customs fees, the bill for fumigating the equipment when it arrived at the port, down to the cost of replacing a single padlock on the shipping container.

As they went over each document, Craig kept a running count of all his unpaid expenses. When the bottom of the stack of papers was reached, he slid the total figure he owed to the government official for approval, pulling his checkbook out of his bag. The official compared the number Craig had written to his paperwork.

"Yes, this and then four hundred more," the official told Craig through Sergio after he went back through the documents.

"What for?" Craig shot me a quizzical look.

"For other expenses." Sergio shrugged as he translated the official's words.

"How did I miss four hundred dollars when I was adding it all up?"

"You didn't," Sergio stated matter-of-factly. Craig shot me another confused look before conferring quietly with Sergio. Should he pay the extra money? Was this normal? Sergio confirmed that the request wasn't out of the ordinary and that we should pay if we hoped to get help with future shipments. But, he told us, there was room for negotiation.

"How about two hundred?" Craig countered. Sergio translated and the government official shook his head.

"He wants at least three hundred," Sergio said, relaying the response.

"Two fifty?" The official thought for a few moments and then nodded, extending a hand for a handshake. Craig wrote a check for the legitimate amount he owed and then counted out cash from his billfold to cover the rest. The check was handed directly over. The cash was paid, quite literally, under the table.

"Do you think I should ask him for a receipt for that?" Craig asked me with a wink.

In the long run, an extra two hundred and fifty dollars was minuscule in exchange for getting tens of thousands of dollars of baseball equipment into the country without being taxed. We still left the meeting bitter anyways, on principle alone.

Our meeting with the bishop was much more pleasant. As soon as we walked into her office in the back of the church, she jumped to her feet to embrace us.

"Craig! Dan! A friend of mine from Masaya just called me," she said, hugging each of us in turn. "She said that the children brought all their new equipment to her house to show her. She was in tears on the phone with me because she was so happy to see the kids so happy."

We had stopped at Masaya on Friday to deliver gear to two youth baseball teams. Although the city is the third largest in Nicaragua, it has historically had very little success producing baseball prospects. Only six baseball players from Masaya have ever played in the minor leagues. Only three have made it that far in the last decade. Only one of those six made it as high as AA-ball. Marlon Avea, the Houston Astros catching prospect, is the only active player from the city currently playing for a team affiliated with the major leagues.

"There's not a lot of opportunity," Avea told me when I asked about his hometown. I had seen it first-hand during our visit, the pure dirt field being battered by a windy dust storm. The kids without uniforms carrying off their new equipment in canvas dog food sacks. The livestock mingling in the outfield. Nothing we had seen suggested we were in a baseball hot spot, despite the size of the city. But, Avea is optimistic about the future in his hometown.

"Baseball is getting more organized there and there's more chance now than before."

Of course, the same can be applied across the

country, both the lack of opportunity and the hope for better days ahead.

"Not very many doors open in Nicaragua," Seattle Mariners prospect Kevin Gadea said as we talked about his experiences in baseball. I had been in Nicaragua when he signed his first professional contract in 2012, facing him on the mound during our first exhibition game at Dennis Martinez's academy. I bunted every at bat after seeing the first mid-90s fastball he threw past me. Seeing might be a loose term. I bunted every at bat after *hearing* the first mid-90s fastball he threw past me.

"I felt so happy knowing that I was getting an opportunity," Gadea said, describing what he felt on the day he signed with Seattle. "I know that in this country, not very many doors open. The day that I pitched against you was the first time in a long time that I felt relaxed while pitching, knowing that I was accomplishing my first goal of signing. I actually threw harder that day than during any of my previous tryouts."

Gadea and Avea are two of a very small number of Nicaraguans who ever take the first step towards the major leagues and sign with a professional team. Hopefully, through our deliveries of baseball equipment to Masaya and other Nicaraguan cities, we played a part in giving more children that opportunity. Even if none of the children we met ever play in the major leagues, if our work brought hope to communities that previously had little, our trip was a success.

As we wrapped up our meeting with the bishop, Craig making sure all bills and expenses the church had taken on to make our project possible were covered in full, we also were wrapping up the baseball portion of our trip. Over ten days, we had brought thousands of pieces of baseball equipment to hundreds of children across the country. We fell short of our goal of completely emptying the warehouse, a chore we realized would have taken months instead of weeks, but Nemesio gladly accepted the job of distributing the remaining gear to teams of all ages around the country.

Our next focus would be the farming projects in the northernmost reaches of the country, an experience Craig repeatedly asserted would be the most impactful part of the trip for me as we drove away from the church and to the airport. Scott Ramsdell, an agronomist from South Dakota and longtime friend of Craig's, was on the next flight into Nicaragua to join us on our trip north.

"Scott is the *jefe* of all things farming here," Craig told me on the way to pick him up, using the Spanish word for boss. Scott had been involved with the farming projects since their inception, taking his experience in agriculture from his family business Dakota Layers in South Dakota and applying it to help Nicaraguan families get access to irrigation, fertilizer, insecticides, and seeds and instructing them directly on how and when to most efficiently use them.

We found Scott at baggage claim, and he immediately impressed me as someone worthy of the *jefe* title. He was no-nonsense, leading with a firm handshake and skipping past all the small talk about how his flight had been to grill Craig about the trip so far and the plan for the next three days. He didn't have much time in the country and was intent on dedicating every moment to the success of Nicaraguan agriculture.

When we got back to our hotel, the 'no' dissolved off his no-nonsense persona, and Scott began teasing and belittling Craig for times long passed. Like Jay, Scott had been friends with Craig for longer than either could remember. With the plan for the next three days established on the drive back to the hotel, Scott was relaxed and affable as we sat by the pool enjoying our nightly round of beers.

As I sat and listened to the banter between the two, an employee from the hotel tapped me on the shoulder.

"Señor, there is a problem with your room." I looked up, concerned. "We believe there is a problem with the water pipes in your bathroom. It smells very bad in there. We have moved you to a new room and are very sorry for the inconvenience."

She held out a new room key to me. I went into my old room to retrieve my belongings and was blown away by a rancid stench as soon as I opened the door.

After sticking my head outside the room to take a deep breath, I re-entered the room intent on grabbing my things as quickly as possible and getting back outside before I passed out from the smell. I tossed my suitcase out the door without even taking the time to zip it up, sweeping all of my belongings from my bed and bedside table into it with one arm, the other clenched firmly over my mouth and nose.

After depositing my suitcase outside, I took another deep breath and headed into the bathroom to retrieve the clothes I had washed and hung to dry on the shower rod and towel rack. I began gagging as soon as I entered the bathroom.

God, I hope this smell doesn't stick to my clean clothes, I thought as I reached to grab the hangers my clothes hung from. My arm brushed against one of my shirts. It was damp to the touch. I stuck my nose to it, afraid of what I'd find.

The stench in my room was not from faulty pipes. It was coming directly from my 'clean' clothes. I thought that the heat would be enough to dry them hanging in my bathroom, but they had sat for two full days now, still soggy and rotting.

After getting more air from outside, I pulled the garbage bag from the trash can in my room, emptying the wrappers and empty water bottles inside into the trash can directly. As quickly as I could, I shoved my putrid clothing into the garbage bag and tied it as tight as I could.

I carried my suitcase and garbage bag of clothes, holding the clothes with my arm extended as far away from me as I could, across the hotel's lobby.

"Pretty bad in there?" Craig asked, seeing the disgusted look on my face.

"They really need to get those pipes fixed," I lied as I headed to my new room trying to decide what in the world I was going to wear for the rest of the trip.

Chapter 12

It took four hours of rural highway to get to Somoto, a small city so close to the Honduran border that my cell phone kept buzzing with messages from my carrier either welcoming me to Honduras or back to Nicaragua depending on where I stood after we arrived. Thankfully, Luis was able to get the truck back to us prior to our departure. It was a long drive early in the morning, made more uncomfortable by the fact that I was wearing soggy re-washed clothes.

Not wanting to spend the next three days in the Mitchell Sluggers youth jersey, I had frantically washed two of the shirts from my garbage bag in my new hotel room's sink, skipping breakfast so I would have something to wear that wouldn't make everyone else in the truck sick. I was wearing one, still wet, hoping that it would dry out on the trip if I kept my window open. The other was tied to my bag in the bed of the pickup, flapping in the wind as we drove.

To call Somoto a city would be giving it a lot of

credit. It was little more than a church, a hotel, a ball field, and a few scattered shops and restaurants linked by uneven cobbled streets.

We dropped our bags off at the only hotel in town, a quaint little colonial compound, the rooms arranged in a square around a garden plaza. With our bags gone, we drove deep into the countryside, long past the last electrical poles. The scenery was near-breathtaking, earthy mountains towering on either side of the bumpy dirt road.

Any breath I had left was taken when I saw the poverty. Small clusters of houses dotted the side of the road, the homes nothing more than clumps of mud stacked on top of each other and dried in the sun. Most of the houses in their entirety, never more than two rooms in total, were smaller than my bedroom had been growing up. Citizens walked the side of the road barefoot, carrying buckets in search of water to bring home. Skinny cattle ranchers drove skinnier cattle down the single-lane road. I had no idea where they were going. It had been miles since I had last seen grass.

In the valleys between the mountains, there was little life beyond the people and the cattle. Small tumbleweed shrubs grew in clumps in dusty pastures. Pathetic fields of corn, the plants looking more like Charlie Brown's Christmas tree than crops, tried to grow out of the dry, cracked earth. Even the sky above seemed pale, like the sun had drained its color.

"Welcome to our farming projects!" Craig said, turning to face me in the back seat. "The families here work together to farm their fields. We help provide them with the seed, the fertilizer, the compost, and the irrigation they need to actually grow something in this climate. Scott teaches them how to use it all so that they will be able to continue to grow crops when we're not here anymore. All of the families who help in the fields share in the harvest."

When we arrived at the first community, over thirty farmers—men, women and children—were crowded around two small steel silos on their hands and knees. A bag of red beans had burst, and the whole community was crawling through the dirt to make sure none were left on the ground. Craig didn't even wait to say hello, dropping to his knees to help. Because the community shared the harvest, each bean left in the dirt was one less for the families to eat.

When the beans had been successfully retrieved, the community showed us their two silos—one six feet tall, the other four—that they had filled with corn during the past harvest. The taller silo was already empty.

While Craig shook hands and exchanged pleasantries with farmers he had met on prior trips, Scott went straight to work, quizzing the farmers on corn prices, harvest dates, and yields. The farmers had been skeptical at first when Scott arrived advocating fertilizers, compost, and irrigation the farmers had never used before. They had farmed the same way using traditional dry land practices their entire lives, and many were unwilling to take the risk of trying something new. A bad harvest would be devastating, the families forced to choose between eating the corn and beans they produced or having seed to plant the next cycle.

When Scott asked the farmers to report on their yields from the bean harvest, it was incredible to listen to. Two farmers who had used completely traditional methods of farming reported that they had produced three and five bags of beans, respectively. A farmer who had used fertilizers suggested by Scott but hadn't had access to irrigation grew twelve bags worth. The farmers who worked on the irrigated and fertilized field had twenty canvas bags of beans stacked proudly next to the silos for the whole community to see. With one hundred pounds of crop in each bag, the difference between traditional methods and Scott's suggestions was thousands of pounds of food for the community.

"It's a simple as this," Craig told me as we listened to Scott discuss with the local farmers, Sergio translating. Noelle, a recent agronomy graduate from the local university, helped explain the more technical points in Spanish. "More families will have more food to eat this year because of the farming projects. You might not get to see the results of the baseball project ever. You'll never know how it improved a kid's life unless they make it to the major leagues. But this, the impact of this is sitting right there in those bags."

He was right. I had thought many times during the trip that the baseball projects felt the same to me as teaching had. While teaching, I knew at the end of the day that I had done something good to help my students, but the real results, beyond a grade on a test, wouldn't materialize for years. The impact of the farming was spread out in front of me, in the bags of beans and on the faces of the local farmers breathlessly telling Scott about their record harvest.

The farmers asked if they could show us their fields, and we followed them away from their meager houses and into the countryside. As we walked, Scott turned to us.

"You know how much they can sell one of those bags for?" he asked. Neither Craig nor I had the answer. "Eight hundred Cordobas. They get eight hundred Cordobas for one hundred pounds of beans. Do you know how much we spent when we stopped at Burger King on the way here? Eleven hundred Cordobas, just on lunch. We just spent more money on a couple hamburgers than these farmers make for months of work plowing, planting, weeding, and harvesting their fields by hand."

The comparison made Craig and I go quiet as we walked out to the field. It made us realize just how little the people of northern Nicaragua had. It made us realize just how much we had.

The difference in monetary value between the traditional fields and the irrigated, fertilized field was incredible: over thirteen thousand Cordobas, close to five hundred US dollars. For the nearly half of all Nicaraguans living on less than a dollar a day, the majority of those families living in the rural north, an extra five hundred dollars would be life-changing. Not only did the farming project put food on the table for the families walking with us to the fields, it allowed them to have an opportunity at an income as well.

"Sustainability is the long term goal here," Scott told me as we walked. The ground was loud beneath us, so dry that it cracked under our shoes. "I'm actually disappointed with their yield. If they weed their fields more regularly and follow our planting and harvest schedule, they should be able to get much more than twenty bags of beans out of that field. We want them to produce enough to feed themselves first, then have left over corn and beans to either plant the following season or sell to buy seed, fertilizer, and anything else their farms may need. In a year or two, it will pay for itself. They won't need us here anymore, especially if more farmers are willing to adapt their practices and use more modern techniques."

The farmers' field was one *manzana* in area (a unit of measurement equal to approximately 1.7 acres). Black garden hose tubing was laid in horizontal rows a few feet apart stretching the length of the field. Small holes had been punctured every few inches in the tubes to allow water to escape. Although the field was empty—the beans had recently been harvested, and the stocks were already tilled under the soil—it was easy to tell the difference between the irrigated dirt and the ground surrounding it. The dirt in the field was soft, almost spongy, in comparison to the sunbaked dirt around it. A central tube ran down the middle of the field perpendicular to the rows of hosing. The main tube ran from the field up the side of a hill bordering the field. A large holding tank sat on top of the hill. A series of solar panels sat at its base next to a well house.

"The well draws the water from the ground. The solar panels provide the power needed to pump the water up the hill to the holding tank. From there, gravity takes over, pulling the water down the hill through the main tube to the field where it is channeled down all the rows of tubing to get to the plants," Scott said, explaining the system to me. It was ingenious, allowing the farmers to water their crops in a region that had no water.

The farmers showed us their sorghum pile, the bland crop they planted around the perimeter of their corn and bean fields to prevent insects and wildlife from destroying their crops. Besides protecting their fields, the sorghum was used to feed their livestock and, in years of poor harvest, the farmers themselves. They had recently harvested the crop and left it in a shoulder-high mound to dry in the sun.

The solar panels and irrigated field

"You should see the field when it's got corn in it. It's the only green thing in this whole valley. You can see it from miles away. It looks incredible from up in the mountains. Just one little square of bright green surrounded by all the dull brown here," Craig told me while inspecting a stock of sorghum from the pile. "When the corn or the beans are getting close to harvest, the farmers guard the field twenty-four hours a day. Can you imagine that? Having to guard your food all day and all night so it doesn't get stolen? That's how bad things are here. Of course, by allowing anyone who helps in the fields to take home a share of the harvest, we're hoping more people will join the project instead of trying to steal from it. More people, more hands, more production, more food."

It seemed like that was exactly what was happening. After visiting the fields, we were introduced to the new families that had joined the project since Scott and Craig's last visit. Five new families had joined after seeing the corn and bean harvests.

We returned to the house with the silos outside, the home of the farmer who owned the land the irrigated field sat on. The house was one of the biggest we had passed. Pieces of straw and rock stuck out of the mud bricks that formed the house's two rooms. A sheet metal ceiling hung above dirt floors. Only one straw bed sat inside for the farmer's entire family.

Scott spoke briefly to the congregation of farmers. He laid out the plan for the following crop cycles, encouraging them to plant vegetables in the field between the corn and bean harvests to supplement their diets and reiterating the need to thoroughly weed the fields to increase production.

Scott had originally come to Nicaragua hoping to help the farmers raise chickens to produce eggs. His project would have added a valuable source of protein to the meager diets in the region that typically consist of corn tortillas, red and black beans, rice if it can be afforded, and any vegetables the families are able to grow in their own gardens.

However, after visiting the communities, he quickly realized how flawed his plan was. The families wouldn't be able to feed their chickens if they couldn't feed themselves. Given the choice between waiting for the chicken to lay an egg tomorrow or not starving tonight, the chicken was always going to be the loser.

So, he had turned his attention to feeding the farmers first. Now with successful harvests under their belt, more and more local families joining the project, and sustainability on the horizon, the egg project was becoming a possibility again.

Broad smiles broke out across the farmers' faces when he told them this. It was almost strange to see, smiles despite the dirt and the poverty. There was a roughness in the people here I hadn't seen in the rest of the country. Their faces, their skin, their hands, their voices were all calloused from years of hunger and hard manual labor under the sun.

The farmers asked Scott general questions about farming: how to apply fertilizer, how deep the seeds should be planted, how much space should be put between rows. Only the men spoke; the females in the group stood listening, holding on to children. One woman raised her hand.

"I would like the chance to talk for the women," she said. She paused before she began speaking again. "Normally only the men are allowed to work here. We stay in our homes with the children and do little else besides clean and tend to our garden. Your project has given us opportunity. Some of us get to work in the fields here, our husbands too stubborn to give up their methods and join the group. When we bring home more food than them..." She tailed off, smiling. Smirks curled the lips of the other women in the group. "Whether we are working in the field or doing something else for the project like bookkeeping, husking the corn, or helping to distribute, we get to do important work now. Thank you, Scott."

Moments like this keep Scott coming back. Often his work can be frustrating, the farmers resisting his advice and plans in favor of outdated farming practices.

"Sometimes it feels like a 'you can lead them to water' situation when they want to stick with old ways. Even though there has been improvement, the yields could be doubled or even tripled if they farmed properly. It's not the farmers' fault. They were given land by the government during the revolution but never taught how to farm it. I'm here to teach them how to farm properly."

Education has become one of Scott's main goals with the farming projects. When he first arrived and was discussing the egg project with local farmers, the farmers expressed disbelief that he planned to only brings hens to the farmers.

"They asked why there were no roosters. They didn't know that you don't need a rooster for a hen to lay eggs."

His goal is to have the farming projects be fully self-sustainable in three years, meaning that the projects will pay for themselves through the sale of the harvests and that the farmers will be able to continue successfully without his help. To do so, he has focused on teaching the farmers directly about agriculture and training local agronomists.

Like Craig, Scott has been an avid traveler throughout his life. A licensed pilot, he often flies himself and his family to countries across Latin America. On a visit to Nicaragua, a young boy approached Scott and asked for a Cordoba, the equivalent of about three cents in US currency. Scott turned the boy down.

"The kid was only asking for one Cordoba. He needed food, and I shunned him," Scott recalls about the moment that spurred him to become active with Helping Kids Round First. When Craig began talking about the possibility of farming projects in Nicaragua, Scott refused to miss the opportunity to go back and help others in need like the young boy.

Although it was a denied request for money that inspired Scott to return to Nicaragua, he's focused on making sure his impact there is greater than dollar bills.

"Many Americans go to other countries and act like they're God. They think they're above the locals because they have money. I don't go to Nicaragua to throw around hundred dollar bills. I go to work directly with the people and to help teach them how they can farm better and produce more food. I don't want to be 'the man'. I want to help provide local agronomists with the resources so that the people will turn to them instead of me."

Partway through the second year of his three-year plan, the farming projects have been successful in many ways. Yields have been significantly increased and will continue to go up as more farmers adopt Scott's practices. The target of self-sustainability by the end of year three looks to be an attainable goal. Inadvertently, the projects have helped provide new roles to the women in the farming communities.

The increased opportunity for women is one of the 'old ways' that Scott is most happy to be helping change.

"Traditionally, the men would never teach women how to farm. Now, many of the women are more productive than the men! The farming projects have helped give women importance and status in their communities they didn't have before."

Indirectly, by turning down one boy's request for a Cordoba, Scott has gone on to help hundreds of Nicaraguan families in ways that will have long-lasting impacts on their lives and communities. Fulfilling a slightly altered version of the proverb, by teaching people how to farm in Nicaragua, he is helping feed them for a lifetime.

Chapter 13

Our second day in Somoto was spent at the home of a poor farmer named Gandhi. His house made the one we had visited the previous day look wealthy by comparison. Gandhi greeted Scott and Craig with a hug. He wore a once-white cowboy hat, an unbuttoned flannel-patterned shirt, torn jeans, and cracked leather boots. The soles of his boots were nearly peeled off, slapping the ground with each step. His shoelaces were frayed and broken.

Looking at the other families and farmers gathered to meet us, Gandhi was the only one wearing shoes, however humble they might have been. The rest were in cheap flip-flop style sandals or bare feet.

The community had been exceedingly skeptical of Scott's farming practices when the first fertilizers and irrigation systems were introduced in their fields. They had butted heads with Scott repeatedly, refusing to abandon the traditional methods of farming they had survived on—however modest that survival was—their entire lives. They refused to weed their fields, insisting that the weeds provided cover for the soil, protecting it from the hot sun. When their fields produced little yield, they simply planted larger areas the next season.

To combat this, Scott had set up a series of test plots in the community's fields. He placed areas farmed with traditional methods next to irrigated and fertilized areas and placed areas with all the weeds removed next to areas with the weeds left in so the farmers could visually see and compare the results of the different methods. Many had started to see the benefit of the modern methods, yet many others remained stubborn through the first harvests of the irrigated field.

When the farmers reported their yields to Scott, the results were even more dramatic than at the first farming community. Fields farmed with completely traditional methods had produced just a single bag of beans each. Instead of switching to the more efficient methods available to them, the farmers had planted eight fields using traditional methods thinking that planting more fields would mean more food. They had eight bags of beans to show for their eight fields.

The single field planted using irrigation and fertilizer produced twenty-five bags of beans. Following the harvest of both the test plots and the fields in the community, many of the families who had previously been skeptical asked to join the cooperative.

At Scott's request, the new families stood and introduced themselves. The first few stated that they joined the farming community after seeing the harvests so that they could learn how to produce that much food for their families. The next family was more frank.

"We joined this community so we wouldn't starve,"

we were told by the father of the family. "We had a poor harvest in our field again this year. We need something to eat."

Another family spoke next.

"No one here has a job. We don't make any money. Our income is food."

The conversation grew even heavier with the next family.

"It's hard to have hope or believe in anything when you are starving. Through coming here and helping us, you have given us hope. Through you, we see God."

Through that point, only men had spoken. Their wives had stood at their side, quietly holding children. When the men ran out of things to talk about, the women seized their opportunity to speak. Many of the women in the group had dressed up for the occasion.

"Before this project, we just waited in the house for our husbands to come home," one told us. "Now we have a purpose and a job. We work as one group, and the men work as another. We have shown them that we can work in the field just as well as they can."

Weeks after we had returned to the United States, it would be conversations like this that stuck out most in Craig's mind. Empowering women had been one of his biggest goals through the donation of softball equipment, but the farming projects had accomplished it on a much more basic and immediate level.

We were given a tour of the farms and fields next. A well, latrine, and safer stoves had been installed by the Lutheran Church in the community, giving the citizens access to water and improving sanitation. As we walked through the farmers' fields, one of the women walked next to me, telling me about her family and the continued drought.

"Most of the families here own land that they could farm, but we can't find any water," she said. "We have to send our kids with buckets long distances to find water, but it's getting harder and harder to find."

The drought was a common topic among the farmers. Most talked about the last time they had seen a true rainy season the way Craig talks about past travels. The good ol' days, times past that were simpler and easier. It may have been just a few years since the drought began but a few years is a long time when there isn't food on the table.

With the irrigation systems and fertilizers, we had been able to offset the effects of the drought. After touring the fields, Scott gathered the farmers to discuss the harvest, assert that a greater yield would be possible if they pulled weeds and followed directions more closely, and lay out the plan for the next planting.

As Scott talked, mangy dogs wandered through the house next to us searching for scraps to eat, their ribs sticking through taught skin like xylophone keys. We had seen the same with the livestock in the surrounding fields, cows and horses so skinny you fear they'd keel over if you got too close.

When the last of the questions from the farmers was answered, we packed up to leave, shaking hands and giving hugs goodbye. Before we could make it to the truck, the farmers herded us to a small table set up outside Gandhi's house. Plates of tortillas made from corn and sorghum, red and black beans, homemade cheese, and coffee picked from nearby trees waited for us.

Offering food to guests is a kind gesture anywhere

in the world, but in a region with such abject poverty, where the farmers work months in the field for no pay besides a bag of corn and beans to bring home to their family, the meal prepared for us was a true sacrifice. It did not go unnoticed. We savored every bite. In all honesty, the food was bland at its tastiest moments, the corn tortillas having little flavor and the sorghum tortillas having even less. But there at a table outside a mud brick house in death valley Nicaragua, every bite was a delicacy.

An average home in the Somoto farming community

As we ate, a pair of young girls approached our table. I expected them to ask for something to eat or for a spare Cordoba, requests we would have gladly accommodated. Instead, they held out handwritten letters to Scott and Craig.

"They wanted to say thank you," their mother told

us. I helped translate the letters.

The first was from an eleven-year-old named Genesis. The letter was full of spelling mistakes, most of the words spelled phonetically. Genesis talked of her two brothers, her favorite color, her church, and her daily life.

"During the week, I help my mom haul water and take care of my little brothers. On Friday, I go to church. On Saturday, I get to go to school."

I couldn't imagine that life at eleven. When I was her age, I was a happy sixth grader. An average day consisted of school, Little League practice, and piano lessons. There was food on the table and in the pantry at all times, dad played catch with me in the front yard, and mom tucked me in at night. My only concerns during the day were whether my older sister was listening in on my phone conversation with my middle school girlfriend and if I would survive feeding our pet goat.

The goat was a real concern. I've never met another animal so filled with hate. Every day when I brought him his food, he would lower his horns and charge at me, ramming me into the fence around his pen and pinning me there until my mother would get home from work and free me. I've never despised anything like I did that goat.

His name was Gregory, and he died on my birthday. My parents pulled me aside during my birthday party and told me the goat had passed away. I hugged them, thinking it was a birthday present. I trouped my whole birthday party outside, and we dug a hole and tossed Gregory in and then had birthday cake. It's still one of the warmest memories of my childhood.

I've digressed. My childhood was comfortable and secure. I had no responsibilities, no cares, no worries. Reading Genesis' letter, the words the bishop had told me during our initial meeting on our first day in the country became more clear. "The children here grow up too fast." At eleven, Genesis was one of the children being sent miles with a bucket in search of water. She was forced to adopt a parental role to her younger brothers so her parents could work the fields in hopes of bringing home enough food at night. Her responsibilities at home limited her education to just one day a week, making it nearly impossible to hope for a brighter future.

We invited the girls to join us at the table and finished our meal in good company. As we prepared to leave after eating, I watched Craig carefully fold the letters and place them into the breast pocket of his loose button-up shirt. They would make another keepsake from the trip to go with his Amazonas hat.

One small positive of the extended drought was that the mountain pass between Somoto and Somotillo, the next farming community we would be visiting, was finally dry enough to be driven safely. Craig had wanted to take the more direct and more scenic route between the two cities for years, but he had always been turned away by roads too slick and muddy.

Instead of driving back through Somoto, south down the highway we had arrived on, west around the mountain range, and back north up to Somotillo, we headed directly up the side of the valley on a one-lane dirt road. Even with the road dry, the altitude soon became dizzying. A mere glance out the window left me double-checking to make sure my seat belt was securely fastened, the road giving way to a precipitous drop just inches from my seat. Despite the beauty of the scenery, the mountains folding around us, I clenched my eyes shut. I had always been afraid of heights.

With Jay back home, Scott was put in charge of the radio.

"What have you got for us, Scott? We've already had the Tallgrass Tour with Jay," Craig asked as Scott plugged his phone into the auxiliary chord on the radio.

"No folk music from me. We're going to be doing an Ed Sheeran afternoon. I've got his whole new CD for you."

I froze. How could sixty-plus-year-old men continue to play music that reminded me so damn much of her? All I needed now was for Craig to pop in a Watsky CD, the rapper I dragged her to see on the world's worst first date. I had known she was a keeper when she jumped around next to me, waving her arms in the air, dancing all kinds of ridiculous throughout the concert even though she had heard his music for the first time on the car ride to the show.

In reality, I had known she was a keeper long before that. I had known the night we met. We sat up just talking, completely unaware and unconcerned with the time, until the sun began rising outside my window. I had known the following day, having known each other for less than twenty-four hours, when she told me she loved me for the first time. I had known every minute and every moment since, up until the day she disappeared.

For our one-year anniversary, I took her to see Ed Sheeran live. We didn't have a date on the calendar for our anniversary in the traditional sense; we simply called a year from the day we met our anniversary. We had been together, by any definition of the word, starting the moment she told me her name.

She had chosen his love ballad Thinking Out Loud as 'our song' early in our relationship and sung it into my ear more times than I could count during our time together. I would always prefer her version, partly because she sang like an angel and mostly because she was one. At the concert, she had clung to me so tight, whispering the lyrics through tears into my ear, knowing I would be leaving in just a few days for the Peace Corps.

I hadn't listened to an Ed Sheeran song since we'd broken up. I love his music and have since long before he was blowing up every radio station, but even the intro chords to his songs turned into daggers, rushing me back to all the moments we had danced arm-in-arm alone in her room to them or sang them obnoxiously to each other in the car.

I knew hearing Thinking Out Loud would hurt, but I was just as afraid to hear his lesser-known ballad Tenerife Sea. The song had always done a better job of describing how I felt for her than 'our song' did. When I was preparing to leave for the Peace Corps, I had decided to try to lessen the sting of me leaving by writing her a series of letters to open while I was away. For six months, I sat down and wrote to her every night before bed, filling nearly two hundred envelopes with letters, pictures, presents, lyrics, mementos, memories, and, generally, my heart and soul. In the very last envelope I filled before leaving, I simply slipped a CD with Tenerife Sea on it, scrawling "A song I wish I wrote about you" on the case.

I kept my eyes closed as we drove, the music making my memories fight in my head. I was no longer in the truck but back in our seats at the concert, sitting so close we should have only needed one ticket. Don't and then Sing pumped through the speakers. I'm A Mess made more sense to me than it ever had before. I could feel her arms wrapped around my waist, her head on my shoulder. When Tenerife Sea began, I opened my eyes, trying to shake her out of my head. My fear of heights couldn't feel worse than the music.

Outside the window, a pair of buzzards circled high over the valley far below us. At first, I let them help me feel sorry for myself. *It's a good thing they can't see me*, I thought. *They'd tear me open because I'm dead inside.*

My conscious slapped me as quick and hard as it could. How could I feel sorry for myself sitting in an air-conditioned truck driving on a beautiful mountain pass halfway around the world from home having seen what I had seen the last few days? In the valley we were driving away from, hundreds of families sat praying for a harvest that would let them sleep comfortably at night, not knowing if there would be food tomorrow. And me, sitting there sad because a song reminded me of a girl. Sure, she was the girl of my dreams, but I had forgotten just how lucky I was to have dreams.

I watched the buzzards circle high in the sky over the valley and the farming projects below. Were they waiting for the livestock? The scrawny dogs? Or were they waiting for the people?

Hopefully, with continued support from Craig and Scott, it will be the buzzards that go hungry.

Chapter 14

I've endured rough nights in poor quarters while traveling before. (Mainly every night I was in Samoa. I started naming the foot-long centipedes I frequently found in my bed.) Somotillo made my most uncomfortable nights feel like they had been spent in five-star resorts. We arrived after dark at the only hotel in town to find it was overbooked. To accommodate us, they pushed two beds into a bathroom and let Craig and me crash there for the night.

I was amazed they were able to fit one bed into the bathroom, let alone two. Craig and I would be getting personal that night, our beds practically on top of one another. One end of my bed was wedged underneath the sink suspended on the wall in the corner. I watched as water dripped from the pipe beneath the sink onto my mattress.

The two beds formed an L, the foot of one touching the foot of the other. Instead of a shower, a blue 50-gallon barrel sat next to the sink, a bowl floating on top to use to pour the water over yourself. A small wall and a shower curtain kept the toilet in the corner partially obscured from view. No wall or curtain could contain the smell.

"Toilet doesn't flush," Craig said, pulling on the handle repeatedly, hoping it would help the smell. "Looks like they just pour water in from the shower barrel to dilute whatever goes in there."

"Let's agree to go to the bathroom in Scott's room."

"That will show him for getting the last hotel room and leaving us in here!"

One single light bulb hung from the ceiling, the dim light adding to the charm of the room. I sat down on my bed, deciding whether to sleep with my head under the sink or uncomfortably close to Craig. The bed was no softer than the ground, and the blanket crumpled up on top wasn't much cleaner. I noticed a small puddle of grimy water on the floor. In the dim light and shadows, the water appeared to be moving, creeping closer to my bed.

I looked closer. The water was definitely moving, if it even was water. I shuddered thinking of the alternatives. To be sure the lighting wasn't playing tricks on me, I pulled my pen out of my notebook and marked on the floor where the water ended. It was still a few feet from my bed.

Thankfully, we didn't have to stay long in our dungeon bedroom. Dinner awaited at the only open restaurant in town. To celebrate the success of the trip as a whole, Craig ordered a bottle of vodka for the table. Scott and Noelle were too busy talking farming to partake, maps and formulas and notes scattered across the table between them. I barely understood a word. They discussed low-cost insecticide alternatives, fertilizer recipes, altitudes and angles necessary for successful gravity-fed irrigation, and sketched topographic maps of the fields they hoped to work with in the future in the margins of their notes. The conversation was muddled further by the constant need for Sergio to translate from Spanish to English and back again and having to plug every measurement into Scott's cellphone to convert standard measurements into metric.

Long after our food was gone, Scott and Noelle continued to work, planning out all of the activities for the farming projects between now and the next time Scott would be able to make the trip down to Nicaragua. I had listened intently at first, trying to pick up as much information as I could, but it became exhausting trying to follow their conversation. Agriculture has a language of its own, and I was clearly less fluent in it than I was Spanish (and I am far, far from fluent in Spanish).

"Alright, I give up, Craig. Pour me a glass, would ya?" I gestured to the vodka bottle.

"Too late!" Craig said. He picked up the bottle and shook it to show it was empty.

"What? Where did it...who?" Craig just smiled. He had consumed the entire bottle by himself. I knew immediately how Ron Burgundy felt when Baxter ate the entire wheel of cheese. *I'm not even mad, that's amazing!*

Throughout the trip to Nicaragua, I was never far from my notebook and pen. I had originally just planned to journal so I could remember the trip years down the road, but after seeing the impact the non-profit was making on the kids and communities, I started asking questions and taking extensive notes everywhere we went. The disaster that followed the bottle of vodka was no exception, "Ooh, the vodka is kicking in! This should be fun!" scrawled up the margin of my notes on agriculture.

It wasn't fun, and that's an understatement.

Now, I'll say right now that I don't blame Craig at all. He worked for over a year to get the trip ready. He logged thousands of miles driving across the Midwest soliciting and collecting donations, hauling truckloads of gear back to South Dakota and unloading it into his warehouse. He sorted and packed it all. He spent weeks learning about international shipping and poring over paperwork and customs forms. He spent thousands of his own dollars throughout the process and purchased the boxes of brand new baseballs and gloves we snuck through the airport in our suitcases himself. He faced multiple roadblocks that threatened the entire project and overcame them all by simply working harder. Then, he flew himself to Nicaragua and spent two weeks in a dark, dirty warehouse in temperatures that hovered near triple digits loading and unloading heavy bags of baseball gear. All of his work had paid off and he deserved to celebrate.

Had the night happened to anyone else but me, I'd have laughed my ass off. Enjoy my pain.

Following dinner, it took two of us to help steer Craig to our cozy hotel bathroom. He kept trying to wander off to see the flowers in the hotel courtyard, despite the fact that it was past eleven at night and pitch-dark out. Eventually, we got him into our room, and I locked the manual deadbolt on the door. It was much too small and would take fine motor skills he didn't have access to at the moment to unlock. He wasn't going anywhere, for better or for worse, unless I opened the door for him.

It was for worse. Definitely for worse. When I turned around after locking the door, he already had his shirt and shorts off, a feat he had accomplished somehow without taking off his Croc sandals. It was a near-comical sight: a sixty-some year old man wearing nothing but whitey-tighty underwear and Crocs squeezed onto a small cot in a dingy Central American hotel bathroom. I probably would have laughed had my bed for the night not been pushed up against his.

There was an uncomfortable amount of man stuffed into the room. Given the choice between sleeping with my face next to Craig's or under the leaky sink, the sink was the much more appealing option. The sink couldn't be worse than pillow talk with a man in Craig's state.

I had to lay down on the far end of my bed and army crawl forward to wedge my face under the sink. I only fit laying on my side, my cheek pressed against the mattress. I got as comfortable as I could and shut my eyes, ready to try my hardest to fall asleep. A drip of water fell from the sink and landed squarely in the middle of my forehead. I could hear Craig breathing heavily from his bed and was glad my face was as far from his hot vodka breath as it could be.

Choosing to put my head on the sink-side of the bed also meant putting my face uncomfortably close to the toilet stall. The smell came in waves and made my eyes water. I clenched my eyes closed as hard as I could and tried to ignore the smell and fall asleep.

A guttural shriek cut through the air in the room, startling me. Out of reflex, my head jerked up, smashing into the porcelain sink. I cursed loudly. Whatever had made the sound was close, probably right outside our room. It was exactly what I needed to deal with at the moment: Craig, the splitting headache now pulsing behind my eyes from the sink, and some sort of beast prowling outside.

The noise came again, lower this time, somewhere between a growl and a moan. Mumbled, slurred words followed. Could this beast talk? Had I hit my head hard enough to be hearing things?

"Dan....Dan...Idon'tfeelsogood." Somehow, the entire sentence was fit into one word. I realized that the beast was in the bed next to mine.

The moaning didn't stop for the better part of an hour. It ranged in tone and volume from desperation to anguish to bad porn soundtrack. He fit words in between moans: grunted pleas, mumbled stories, occasionally my name. A few times, he laughed. The laughter was the most unsettling part: loud, cackled scary-movie howling shrill enough to make my headache burn.

After an hour of constant noise, he pieced a sentence together.

"Dannn...I'm going to throw up." *Awh, shit.* I tried to jump out of my bed, partly to try to find him something to puke into and mainly to get the hell out of the way. Of course, I hit my head on the sink again in my haste.

I searched the room, holding my head, stumbling from the darkness and the dizziness. Conveniently, there was no garbage can in the room.

"Huuurry," I heard Craig beg. The only container I could find in the room was the bowl floating on top of the shower barrel. I grabbed it, water splashing out of it onto my chest, and shoved it into Craig's hands. I barely had my hands out of the way when he began to vomit. I realized there was no way the small bowl was going to have room to fit an entire bottle of vodka and his dinner.

"Craig, we gotta get you to the toilet." He couldn't muster more than a nod. He lumbered to his feet, taking two tries to get himself up off his bed. I guided him towards the toilet stall pulling on his arm. He didn't make it, his hands rushing to his mouth to try and keep the next wave inside. He turned and unloaded into the shower barrel.

"Ooooof." Relief was in his voice. "Now that feels better." He splashed water on his face to rinse his mouth and returned to his bed. A delicious mix of odors, the shit smell coming from the toilet and the new vomit scent from the shower barrel, waited for me back in my bed. With his belly empty, Craig finally stopped moaning and fell asleep.

Unfortunately, he snored much louder than he had moaned. I tried to combat the noise by putting my iPod in and turning it up as loud as I could stand. No luck. Even pushing two pillows over my head didn't block out the noise, although it did help replace the smell in the room with the musty odor of unwashed pillow case.

I wasn't the only one Craig was keeping up. Sometime after two in the morning, there was a loud pounding on our door and multiple voices from outside shouted "Cállate!", 'shut up!' in Spanish. Craig only snored louder, as if mocking them in his sleep.

When the snoring finally abated, fading from a noise I endearingly dubbed "elephant mating call" in my notes to the much more pleasant "hibernating bear", there was sunlight coming in under our door. To me, it was the light at the end of the tunnel.

"Craig, wake up. It's morning." We had another full day of farming ahead of us.

"Go on without me. I might have to sit this one out." His voice was raspy. He sat up in his bed and his eyes immediately became wide. He made a dash for the toilet again. I didn't wait to see if he made it, getting out of the room as fast as I could. As I closed the door behind me, my eyes trying to figure out the bright sunlight outside, he was either puking or choking a pig to death in the room. Both make the same sound, I think.

Update: I checked back after breakfast. The water on the floor definitely moved.

Chapter 15

I don't tell that last story to disparage Craig or take anything away from his character or work. At the end of the day, he is human like anyone else; he just spends the entire day leading up to it working tirelessly to help others. He would be the first to tell you that he is not a saint and never has been. He is incredibly honest to and about himself. That was one of the qualities that endeared me to him most. The man has devoted his life to helping others yet seeks no credit for the impact he makes. He is not interested in recognition or praise. He actually gets bashful and deflects credit to those who have helped him if you try, minimizing his role in a process that would be impossible without his dedication and tireless work. If anyone deserved to celebrate and have a little fun at the end of our trip, it was him.

Plus, it makes for a heck of a story, one more amusing travel anecdote at the bottom of a lifetime's long list of them for him. The only bitterness I hold from the night exists simply because he didn't share any of the vodka with me.

We finished our trip in Nicaragua with a visit to the future farming project in Somotillo. Craig found a way to rally, refusing to miss the chance to see the location of the new project and to see his longtime friend Pastor Hairston. For years, they had stayed at the pastor's home on their visits to Somotillo, staying up long into the night singing, dancing, and playing guitar. The pastor, who I was introduced to at breakfast, was an incredible man, leading seven services each weekend, the final of which he biked three hours to each Sunday afternoon.

Pastor Hairston had helped pick out the community that most needed and was most suitable for a new farming project in Somotillo. The Lutheran Church had recently dug a well in the community, giving the farmers a water supply for irrigation.

With Scott in the lead, we were shown the two locations the farmers had identified as possible homes for their irrigated field. The first was an almost perfectly level clearing, naturally free of rocks and debris. The other was a sloping swath of land marred by boulders and tangled trees.

"You're not going to like hearing this," Scott told the farmers. "The first field is perfect. Flat, level, good soil. But, there's not a hill nearby that will make it possible for our gravity-fed irrigation to work. The slope on the second field, though, will work perfectly."

He took altitude readings with a cell phone app on both fields, explaining the necessary drop of elevation for the irrigation to be successful, showing that the slope on the second field would make it possible for the water to reach all corners of the field.

"It's going to take a lot of work to get this field

ready," he told them. "But, it will work."

The farmers did not seem pleased. They had already begun tilling the flat field in anticipation of our visit. But, they assured Scott they would begin work on the new field immediately.

Scott showed the farmers how to take a soil sample, taking slices of dirt from all across the field to get an average composition of the soil for the entire field. It took a pickaxe to break through the hard, dry ground. I didn't want to think about how much work it would take the farmers to plow the field manually. Scott demonstrated the sampling process himself, using a shovel to remove a diagonal chunk of dirt from the ground, and then let the farmers practice. He left some of the samples with Noelle to be tested in Nicaragua and put some in an empty water bottle for himself. He would sneak it through security at the airport to be tested in his labs in South Dakota. Once he knew the chemical composition of the soil, he would design a tailor-made fertilizer for the field to ensure the soil received the nutrients it was lacking to best support crop growth.

While Scott talked to the farmers, helping them develop a plan for field preparation, I was assigned the job of taking GPS readings in all corners of the field to allow Scott to accurately map the field remotely when he returned home. I wandered the field, taking screenshots of the GPS on my phone at its farthest reaches. I used Snapchat to take a picture of the entire field and label where I had taken readings at.

Following the visit at the new farming project, we made the long drive back to Managua. After the four hour trip, Sergio dropped us off at the Best Western

Hotel next to the airport. After our night in the comfy confines of the hotel bathroom, Craig had decided that we'd earned a night of luxury and hot showers.

We were within walking distance of the airport, so we bid Sergio farewell outside the hotel. For two weeks, he had been with us from early morning until late into the night. Nothing we had done would have been possible without him. I knew a handshake and a thank you would not come close to sufficing, but it was all I could offer.

Once inside our hotel room, Craig turned to me. "So, what do you think?"

I knew he was asking generally about the non-profit, about the projects, about the people, about what we had accomplished.

"I think this room is a bit too comfortable," I said, gesturing to the pair of king-sized beds, the air conditioning unit, and the flat screen TV. "I think I'll sleep under the sink in the bathroom tonight."

We both laughed. Craig tried again.

"Will you be back?"

How could I not? I couldn't imagine how I could go home and simply resume my life in good conscience having met the people, seen the fields (both baseball and farms), and experienced firsthand the overwhelming good Helping Kids Round First was doing in Nicaragua.

Twenty-four hours later, I was home. We flew Managua to Atlanta, Atlanta to Sioux Falls, and then I drove the rest of the way back to Minnesota. My mother and my golden retriever were waiting up for me when I walked in the door.

"It was good," was all I could muster when Mom

asked how the trip had been. I would need a lot more time and a lot more words to try and explain the trip to anyone.

I waited a few weeks to let the trip sink in before contacting Jay and Craig to hear their reflections about the trip. Jay was his typical affable self when I called.

"It was a great trip, but they're all great trips for me," he said. We talked about prior trips, back when it was just him and Craig and whatever equipment they could carry in their suitcases, and how different this trip had been with the container and warehouse of gear. It had been a different trip in many ways. The emphasis on softball and opportunity for women was a welcome change, something Jay was proud to be a part of. This trip had been more a grind than any previous, with less downtime and constant movement to and from the warehouse and the communities. He was amazed by all the help we had gotten from our Nicaraguan counterparts.

"It's so cool to be so connected with the locals. They're happy with what we bring to Nicaragua and want us to keep doing what we're doing. Without their help, none of this happens," he told me as we talked about Sergio, Orvin, Luis, and all the others we'd received help from.

"One of the most rewarding things for me is getting to see the people we've met in the past, being able to form relationships and true friendships so far from home. We met so many new people on this trip, it makes me excited for the future."

The future of Helping Kids Round First is worth being excited for to Jay.

"This is just the start," he told me when I asked

what was next for the non-profit. "Getting the first container shipped to the country is a big deal. Now we know how to do it, how to pack it, how to do the paperwork, and will be able to do it again with more baseball gear and with hospitals. It makes so many other things possible going forward. We're just getting started, especially with Craig in charge. This is what he does every day, and this will be something that keeps going. For me, it's not a question of if we keep going to Nicaragua, it's a question of how big our operation can get. How many people can we help? It's exciting to be a part of."

Craig was equally bullish about the future of Helping Kids Round First.

"Our goal for the trip was to distribute baseball equipment to as many kids as possible, and I feel like we accomplished that. I wanted to establish softball contacts and help teams get started, and we were able to start doing that. It was a very positive trip. We're already thinking about our next trip. We just sent down the money the farmers need to purchase the seed and fertilizer for their upcoming corn crop. We're contacting more and more agricultural businesses to help us expand and start more farming projects. The first hospital will be on its way soon. We're going to take this to the next level."

Craig has lost track of how many trips to Nicaragua he's taken, but this trip will be one he doesn't forget.

"Getting the first container down there makes everything possible going forward. I've never been on a bad trip to Nicaragua, but this one was special to me. I wanted to help women get more opportunities through softball, and I feel we started to do that. But more so, I will never forget those female farmers up in Somoto thanking us for giving them an opportunity to have a job in the fields and talking about how they used to just wait for their husband to come home every night, and now, now they have valuable jobs in the community. Obviously, it's all valuable—the baseball gear, the farming projects, all of it—but it's moments like that that make me sure this is what I want to do with my life."

For me, I'm still not sure if I've fully processed the trip. This book has been my way of reflecting on what I saw and experienced and was a part of. I definitely didn't go to Nicaragua with the intention of writing a book. Heck, I don't think I went to Nicaragua with any intentions at all besides getting myself as far away from my problems as I could.

In the airport on the way home, Craig told me to give him a call anytime if I wanted to be a part of Helping Kids Round First going forward. It's one of his brilliant business tactics. When he calls or meets with a donor to explain the work the non-profit does, he always gets asked the same question: "How much do you want?" He always tells them he doesn't want money. He would rather the donor come to Nicaragua, see and be a part of the projects, and then decide if it's something they would like to be a part of or support in the future. He lets the work speak for itself.

And it spoke to me. I put a lot of thought into how I could help going forward. As an unemployed 23-year-old, there wasn't much I could do monetarily to support Helping Kids Round First. As much as I wished it was, it wouldn't be viable for me to keep going back to

Nicaragua on Craig's near-monthly trips. But, I could write.

So, write, I did. I spent so many days in the same corner table of the same little coffee shop that they should have started charging me rent. Other customers started asking me questions thinking I worked there. The people that did work there started dropping little hints about another coffee shop down the street that maybe I'd like to check out. I didn't blame them. I'd wander in sometime during the morning, order a single small black coffee, the cheapest thing on the menu, and make a day out of it, not leaving until the evening.

After many hours and dozens of bitter cups of dark roast, I hope I've done the trip justice. I left looking to run away and to find my way back to baseball and came back with so much more. For two weeks, we went far beyond baseball, both in the literal sense with our softball, farming, and hospital projects, but also less tangibly, with the friendships and relationships we formed.

For more information on Helping Kids Round First and to find out what you can do to be a part of future projects, please check out:

www.helpingkidsroundfirst.org

Epilogue

I got home and met up with her. To say that the coffee date we scheduled when I got back stateside didn't go well would be an egregious understatement. Neither of us were ready to see the other, and to call it a disaster would probably be too cheerful of a description. Heck, the original outline for this epilogue simply read:

Misery, heartbreak, etc. End on a low note! The good guy doesn't get the girl! Love isn't real! You don't matter!

So you can see where my head was at immediately afterwards. I was so shook-up and heartbroken that night that I tearfully shoved a few handfuls of clothes into the backseat of my car and left Minnesota before the sun was up the following morning.

Even with time and space between us, the situation will continue to break my heart. That young woman is positively and unequivocally the best human being I have ever met. I probably seemed bitter and jaded at times in the preceding pages, and it may be true, but I know the reason I was willing to sacrifice so much to be with her was because she was so overwhelmingly worth it. She was worth giving up my dreams for because she was so much better than they were.

It's a shame that sometimes it just doesn't work out between two good people for reasons completely out of their control. But that's life. There are a lot of hurt feelings on my end, but not hard feelings, and my respect for her will never waver.

It took me way too long to be able to say that and mean it. I spent so much time making things worse, and now it's time to make sure something good comes out of it. I know I never would have gone to Nicaragua had things not turned out the way they did between us. You would not be holding this book (for better or for worse), and any new interest in the wonderful work done by Helping Kids Round First would not have been generated.

For me for now, there's a warm bed in my sister's basement that I'm allowed to stay in if I babysit every once in a while. I'm typically more excited than the kids on those nights when duty calls. For a few hours, I get all the Veggie Tales, mac and cheese, whiffle ball, juice boxes, crayons, and Nerf guns that I can handle. I've tossed the whole idea of going 'beyond baseball' out the window, diving headfirst back into the game. I've been fortunate to have a few of the interviews conducted for this book published as feature articles on a host of different baseball news sites. I was so determined (or desperate, desperate is probably the right word) to find a job within the game, that I showed up at the tryouts to be bat boy for a local minor league team. They took one look at me, wearing a tie and clutching a stack of my resumes and business cards, and politely told me they were looking for someone younger, say, middle school. The good folks at World Baseball Experience have allowed me to be a part of their mission to put baseball on the map around the world. I have no idea where I'll be by the time you read this, but I'm excited about the possibilities.

I know wherever it ends up being, it will be with a warm spot in my heart for Helping Kids Round First and Nicaraguan baseball. I've been incredibly pleased to be able to catch up with some of the communities we visited on our trip. Johnny Alvarez is continuing to pursue his dream of starting a baseball foundation to help train Nicaraguan youth for a career in baseball. He's aptly called his project Working For A Dream and has helped spearhead the distribution of the baseball gear that remained in the warehouse following our trip. On Omatepe, Efrain has used the gear he received to not only outfit his own teams, but to start leagues for children across the island. In the first such league, the first games were just played, and the second league will begin in May.

Stateside, Craig has Helping Kids Round First gunning towards the "next level". With more and more people coming on board with the mission, it appears likely four separate non-profits will be formed out of the original organization. One will handle baseball equipment donations, one will be devoted to softball, Scott will lead the farming non-profit as they expand to new communities, and the burgeoning hospital project will comprise the last.

Over one hundred and fifty generous donors contributed to make our trip a possibility. In the time it took me to write this book, two more groups traveled to Nicaragua to continue Helping Kids Round First's mission and to help provide more opportunities to boys and girls through sport, increase the accessibility of sustainable agriculture to families, and improve healthcare outcomes across Nicaragua. With the growth of Helping Kids Round First and the continued success of their efforts to help Nicaragua, I hope the donor list will continue to grow.

Helping Kids Round First

23075 SD Hwy 13
Flandreau, SD 57028
www.helpingkidsroundfirst.org

International Baseball Academy Central America

Find out more by searching *International Baseball
Academy of Central America* or *International Baseball
Academy* on Facebook or by contacting Bob Oettinger
at: cofbob@gmail.com

Orvin's Realty
Orvin Dublon
orvinsrealty.com

Working For A Dream
Johnny Alvarez
johnnyalvarez86@yahoo.com

To listen to Tallgrass:
www.tallgrassband.com

ABOUT THE AUTHOR

Daniel Venn (above, center) is a Minnesota native and Colorado resident. He is the author of Beyond Baseball, a licensed educator, and a terrible dancer. He owns one of the world's largest collections of ugly neckties and rarely matches his socks.

www.DanVenn.com

88923082R00115

Made in the USA
San Bernardino, CA
19 September 2018